What people are saying about *The Archer and the Arrow*

Most preachers learn to preach from preachers who have been used by God to convert, mature, and train them. Some of this learning is conscious, some is unconscious. So this book is important, as it articulates the preaching of Phillip Jensen, whose teaching of the Bible has been of significant influence in Australia and overseas.

The book clarifies the key features of his preaching: gospel-focused, biblical, theological, passionate, loving, and pastorally applied; and it suggests ways in which we should gain the same strengths in our preaching. Highly recommended.

> **Peter Adam**
> Former Principal, Ridley College, Melbourne, Australia

Preaching is the lifeblood of the local church. God not only forms his church through his word, he also grows, strengthens and matures his church through his word. This is an outstanding book by one of the world's foremost preachers. It is essential reading for any would-be Bible teacher.

> **William Taylor**
> Rector, St Helen's Bishopsgate, London, UK

Phillip Jensen has been both faithfully and provocatively preaching God's word for decades. Here he tells us how. His observations are keen, his suggestions convicting, his speaking plain. (And he also finally explains for us why most commentaries are so useless to the preacher!)

> **Mark Dever**
> Pastor, Capitol Hill Baptist Church, Washington DC, USA
> President of 9Marks

I remember a journalist once describing Phillip's preaching as being "like a submarine commander addressing his sailors". I've always thought that was close to the mark. For over 30 years I've heard Phillip preach the Bible as it is—a matter of life and death. This book is gold, and gives us decades of prayer and thought and practice in how to preach the Scriptures as the very words of God.

> **Al Stewart**
> Director, Fellowship of Independent Evangelical Churches, Australia

Having gained so much from Phillip Jensen's preaching, I am delighted that his thoughts and instruction on the preacher's task are now in print. They are characteristically rooted in Scripture, radical, challenging and inspiring, and will be a great help to all preachers—from the novice to the veteran.

Vaughan Roberts
Rector, St Ebbe's Church, Oxford, UK

The disciple-making vision of *The Trellis and the Vine* will only be realized through the kind of fearless, Bible-driven proclamation of the gospel that has been the hallmark of Phillip Jensen's ministry. For over 20 years I watched him train a generation of young preachers during their ministry apprenticeship. This brilliant book now distils this wisdom for every preacher and would-be preacher.

Colin Marshall
Author, *The Trellis and the Vine*, Sydney, Australia

About the authors

Phillip Jensen is an internationally renowned preacher and evangelist. He is the author of the well-known *Two Ways to Live* gospel presentation, as well as numerous books and Bible study materials, including *The Coming of the Holy Spirit*. He currently serves with Two Ways Ministries in Sydney, Australia. Phillip and his wife, Helen, have three children and thirteen grandchildren. For more resources by Phillip Jensen, visit **phillipjensen.com**.

Paul Grimmond serves as the Dean of Students at Moore Theological College in Sydney where he has helped to develop the preaching training program for pastors in training. He loves working with students and pastors alike to see them grow in their faithfulness and confidence in speaking God's word with conviction, wisdom and grace. Paul is married to Cathy and they have three adult children.

The Archer and the Arrow

PREACHING THE VERY WORDS OF GOD

PHILLIP D. JENSEN
AND **PAUL GRIMMOND**

SYDNEY · YOUNGSTOWN

The Archer and the Arrow
© Phillip Jensen and Matthias Media 2010

All rights reserved. Except as may be permitted by the Copyright Act, no part of this publication may be reproduced in any form or by any means without prior permission from the publisher. Please direct all copyright enquiries and permission requests to the publisher.

Matthias Media
(St Matthias Press Ltd ACN 067 558 365)
Email: info@matthiasmedia.com.au
Internet: matthiasmedia.com.au
Please visit our website for current postal and telephone contact information.

Matthias Media (USA)
Email: sales@matthiasmedia.com
Internet: matthiasmedia.com
Please visit our website for current postal and telephone contact information.

Scripture quotations are from the ESV® Bible (The Holy Bible, English Standard Version®), copyright © 2001 by Crossway, a publishing ministry of Good News Publishers. Used by permission. All rights reserved. The ESV text may not be quoted in any publication made available to the public by a Creative Commons licence. The ESV may not be translated into any other language.

ISBN 978 1 922980 44 1

Cover design and typesetting by Lankshear Design.

Contents

Preface	5
1. The oracles of God	11
2. My aim is to preach the gospel	21
3. Preaching the gospel by expounding the Bible	37
4. On the importance of feathers	65
5. The archer and the target	85
6. To those God has given me to love	99
7. The risks the preacher takes	107
Appendices	117
Appendix I: The strategy of God	119
Appendix II: Preach the negative as well as the positive	135
Appendix III: Tips for young preachers	145

Preface

In the summer of 1990, I walked onto the campus of the University of New South Wales for the first time. I was a new Christian and I was expecting university to challenge my faith. It did, but not necessarily in the ways I'd assumed; God was preparing the way. As I walked along the pathway to the enrolments centre, a fellow student introduced himself and asked if I was a Christian. I told him that I was. His next question was the most obvious question in the world, although I didn't realize it at the time: "Would you like to study the Bible while you are on campus?"

Several weeks later, I found myself sitting in a packed lecture theatre, listening eagerly to an hour-long sermon on the opening verses of Romans. The preacher, who I'd never heard of before, was a man named Phillip Jensen. His preaching was clear, winsome, challenging, theologically rich and exegetically deep—although words like 'theological' and 'exegetical' meant nothing to me at the time. I just knew that I liked it. Here was someone who preached with crystal clarity what God was saying in the Scriptures. Every week, I walked away convicted of my need for Jesus and the importance of trusting him in everything. Every sermon reshaped my understanding of God, myself, and the world that I lived in.

In the coming months and years, God used Phillip's preaching to turn my whole life around, just as he had used it in the lives of hundreds of others before, and has used it countless times since. Among many other things, I learned from Phillip that the Bible is the unified account of God's dealings with his creation, and that it reveals his plans for the world. I came to understand why Jesus' death and resurrection stand at the heart of human history and as the centrepiece of God's self-revelation. And for the first time in my Christian life, I realized that the Bible could be read and understood by anyone willing to obey the God who speaks through it.

Perhaps more than anything else, I learned that Jesus' death and resurrection purchased my life for God. My life was not for my own pleasure; it existed for the glory of my heavenly Father. The result was a career change—I left medicine behind for the folly of preaching the eternal gospel to a needy world. I was not alone. Phillip's preaching continues to raise up a generation of preachers for the cause of Christ. Without doubt, he has been a once in a lifetime preacher, appointed by God to achieve remarkable things for his kingdom.

The purpose of this book is to make some of Phillip's wisdom about preaching available to a wider audience—wisdom acquired over almost four decades of faithful biblical ministry.

In God's kindness, that wisdom has been sharpened and refined by the events of the past few years. While Phillip has spent a lifetime teaching people to preach, for the past five years or so he has had a more formal role in teaching new theological graduates how to preach. This has involved what Phillip describes as "a move from unconscious competence to conscious competence". It's a phrase that requires a little explanation.

In acquiring any new skill, there are a number of stages involved in the learning process. You begin by being unconsciously incompetent—that is you can't do something and you're not even aware that you can't do it. For example, when you were a teenager, you may well have wanted to learn to drive a car while being blissfully ignorant of your inability. It was only when you tried to drive for the first time that you moved from unconscious incompetence to conscious incompetence—that is, to knowing that you didn't know how to do it.

Of course, the good thing about being consciously incompetent is that it motivates you to learn. You ask questions. You try to break the task down, and practise it bit by bit. Over time, through persistence and hard work, you gradually move to conscious competence—you can finally do what you've been trying to do. But somewhere along the line, as you practise your newfound skills over and over again, conscious competence gives way to unconscious competence. You don't need to think about driving any more; it just happens naturally. You can hold a conversation with the person beside you or sing along to the radio—all without thinking about what needs to happen with the clutch and the gearstick.

The problem is that once you are unconsciously competent, it can be very difficult to share your skills with someone else. You find that you can't quite tell them how you do it—you just do it. The process of teaching another person involves intentionally moving from unconscious competence back to conscious competence. That has been the process Phillip has been going through in recent years as he has sought to teach others to preach. He has had to stop and think about how and why he does what he does, so that he can pass on some of the important lessons to others.

That's where this book began. Phillip and I started working on the project together, with the aim that I would fashion Phillip's growing reflections on preaching into something accessible to anyone interested in growing as a preacher.

Hopefully the result is theologically and biblically clear, as well as practically challenging and useful. Of course, it is not all that could be said about preaching, and not even all that Phillip would want to say about preaching. For those who want to chase up some of his further thoughts on preaching, please see the additional articles, audio and video available at phillipjensen.com.

Now it says on the title page that the book is written by both of us. What that really means is that Phillip did the thinking and had the ideas, and I worked out how to organize them into chapters and write them down. Indeed at a couple of points in this section where the discussion drops into the first person, it's Phillip talking, not me (such as when he describes the week he spent preparing a sermon on Matthew 5).

But before we move on, there is perhaps one more question to answer. Who exactly am I?

I am a preacher whose life and ministry owes a great debt, under God, to Phillip's friendship and preaching. I have been listening to Phillip in various contexts for the past 20 years. I did a two-year ministry apprenticeship under his leadership at the University of New South Wales in the mid 1990s, and then returned from training at Moore Theological College in 2001 to work as an assistant minister under him.

In God's sense of humour, I was then given the task of following him in the pulpit at Campus Bible Study and Unichurch at the University of New South Wales. His preaching has literally changed my life. And I have spent the past 10 years trying to put into practice what I have learned from him. My aim has not been to copy him, but to learn to preach in the light of the principles that I have learned from him, all the while acknowledging that God has created me as an entirely different personality.

Given my long association with Phillip as a colleague and friend, and some limited experience as a preacher in my own right, I was apparently a logical choice to work on this project with him. It has been an honour and joy to be involved. Over the past 12 months I have spent many hours in conversation with Phillip and others who have learned from him, with the goal of putting this book together. I pray that it will encourage and inspire a new generation of preachers to love Jesus and to preach his words to a world that so desperately needs them.

But let me finish with an important warning. I don't expect that you will be so crass as to read this book hoping to be just like Phillip. However, if you're anything like me, hidden away in the quiet recesses of your heart is the longing to change the world by your preaching. It is all too easy to read a book like this with that terrible mixture of longing for Christ's glory and for personal recognition and renown.

So let's remind ourselves at the beginning. This book does not contain five simple steps to preaching like Phillip. Nor is it the promise that, even if God has given you the gifts to be able to preach like him, your ministry will have the same visible effect. This book is not about Phillip's ability to keep hundreds of people listening to him preach for an hour and a half at a time, although God has given him the capacity to do that. Nor is it a book about how to grow a large church through your preaching, though God might use what is learned and practised as a result of reading it to grow his church in amazing ways. It is rather a book about what it means *to preach the very words of God*.

May reading it cause you to delve deeply into God's word, so that you might grow more and more as a faithful preacher of God's power, glory and grace, to his eternal honour.

Paul Grimmond
2010

Chapter 1

The oracles of God

This book is all about preaching. And as we begin, we need to ask the obvious question: What do we mean by 'preaching'?

For most people, 'preaching' refers to the monologue that takes place from some more or less sturdily constructed device for holding notes, at roughly the same time every Sunday morning, amongst the gathering of God's people. It involves a certain kind of person, with particular gifts, often with specific educational qualifications and a distinct mode of communication.

It is understandable that we call this activity 'preaching'. After all, we live in a world where preaching isn't confined to the Sunday sermon. There are Muslim preachers and Jewish preachers and even atheist preachers. Preaching is a perfectly good word to describe what each of these preachers does, if for no other reason than it's hard to find another English word that describes the activity of declaring a message in a monologue to a group of listeners.

But this creates a problem for us. The common use of 'preaching' to describe what happens from the pulpit has the potential to derail our discussion of preaching before it has begun. If preaching is about the pulpit monologue, then the person who wants to become a better preacher might easily be persuaded to read books about hints and tips on how to hold an audience. Questions of rhythm, pace and timing become essential. The craft of preaching submits to the art of oratory. Rhetorical skill and comedic genius become the essential weapons in the preacher's arsenal. But this is not biblical preaching.

It's not that a preacher's ability to communicate is entirely irrelevant, as we shall see in chapter 5. But biblical preaching is not defined by the gift of communication. In the Scriptures, preachers are not remarkable because of their charisma or dramatic ability. Rather, they are commended for speaking God's truth.

Moses on Mount Sinai was not called upon to embellish the message with his own personal touches but to speak what God told him to speak. "So Moses came and called the elders of the people and set before them all these words that *the Lord had commanded him*" (Exod 19:7). Samuel was not required to keep the people from boredom by his judicious selection of witticisms, but stood before kings and commoners alike to remind them of God's precious commandments and promises—"So Samuel told *all the words of the Lord* to the people who were asking for a king from him" (1 Sam 8:10). Ezekiel's mouth was spiritually muzzled so that he could only open his mouth to utter what the Lord had spoken—"I will make your tongue cling to the roof of your mouth, so that you shall be mute and unable to reprove them, for they are a rebellious house. But when I speak with you, I will open your mouth, and you shall say to them, *'Thus says the Lord God'*" (Ezek 3:26-27).

Throughout the Bible, the essence of speaking God's word is faithfulness to the message as it has been received from God. Even the Lord Jesus came not to speak his own words but the words of his Father in heaven (John 14:24). And when Jesus sent his apostles into the world, it was to preach the message that he gave them—"teaching them to observe all that *I have commanded you*" (Matt 28:20). They were to speak the very same message that Jesus himself had received from his Father (John 16:12-15).

That is why the apostle Paul speaks so often of his own ministry in terms of stewardship (1 Cor 4:1-2, 9:17; Eph 3:2; Col 1:25). Paul has been given something by God that is not his own—it is God's gift for the sake of others. And the most important thing that he can do as a steward of the mysteries of God is to pass them on as clearly and faithfully as he can. As Paul himself puts it:

> This is how one should regard us, as servants of Christ and stewards of the mysteries of God. Moreover, it is required of stewards that they be found trustworthy.
> (1 Cor 4:1-2)

The distinguishing feature of a good steward is that they be found trustworthy—that they deliver in pristine condition whatever has been entrusted to them.

The *Mona Lisa* is probably the world's most famous painting. It currently resides in a purpose-built, bullet-proof case in the Louvre. It is considered so precious that it has only been exhibited outside of the Louvre twice in the last century. In 1963, it was displayed for a time in the National Gallery of Art in Washington D.C., and then in the spring of 1974 it was hung in the Tokyo National Museum.

Can you imagine what might have happened if those responsible for delivering the painting decided that the *Mona Lisa* was a little short of artistic merit? What if they had whipped out a brush in transit and added a nice floral pattern to the border or updated the dress to the duck-egg blue fashion of the day? "We thought it was a little dreary and we wanted to brighten it up a little." This would not have been an acceptable excuse. Their job wasn't to improve the painting, but to deliver it in its original condition.

How much more with the word of God!

Peter expresses it clearly in his instructions to the believers scattered amongst the dispersion:

> The end of all things is at hand; therefore be self-controlled and sober-minded for the sake of your prayers. Above all, keep loving one another earnestly, since love covers a multitude of sins. Show hospitality to one another without grumbling. As each has received a gift, use it to serve one another, as good stewards of God's varied grace: whoever speaks, as one who speaks oracles of God; whoever serves, as one who serves by the strength that God supplies—in order that in everything God may be glorified through Jesus Christ. To him belong glory and dominion forever and ever. Amen.
> (1 Pet 4:7-11)

The goal of life for those living in the last days is the glory of Christ. And Christ is glorified when we live self-controlled, prayerful, loving, servant-hearted lives in which we speak the very oracles of God to one another. The incredible thing here is that the command to speak as one who speaks the oracles of God does not just apply to the 'preacher' but to whoever speaks amongst the congregation of God's people. For all of God's people, everywhere, the challenge is to speak to each other as those who speak the very truths of God and nothing less. Whether we speak one to another over a meal or one to a thousand from the pulpit on Sunday morning, the aim for all Christians is to speak God's truth in order that we might all be encouraged to live for the glory of Christ as we await his return.

What, then, is the essence of preaching? It is not related to the number of people we speak to, nor is it related to our ability to communicate. The essence of preaching is passing on the message as we have received it—that is what it means to speak the very oracles of God.

Clarifying the confusion

And so we find ourselves in a rather awkward place. In a book that is quite clearly about preparing and delivering sermons, we have just suggested that sermons and preaching are not synonymous. What should we make of that?

The point is that although preaching shouldn't be limited to sermonizing, Christian sermons must be defined by a biblical understanding of preaching. Biblical preaching is about communicating God's thoughts and not our own. And so we preach biblically whenever and wherever we declare the word of God to each other. In fact, sometimes there may even be more preaching happening over morning tea than from the pulpit, if dozens of conversations revolve around sharing God's words of encouragement and rebuke with one another. Sermons, in other words, are a subset of a larger activity—the activity of proclaiming God's word to one another, and from one generation to the next.

Preaching is an activity that all are called on to perform. But it is also an activity particularly given to the prophets, evangelists, pastors and teachers within the congregation of God's people. By framing the issues in this way, we remind ourselves that preaching doesn't begin with the aim of preparing a helpful and interesting message that will, at the very least, keep people from their morning siesta—even if it doesn't manage to restrain them from rampant day-dreaming. That is not the heart of preaching. The heart of preaching is declaring what God has said.

The rest of this book will concentrate on the process of preparing and preaching the weekly sermon, and will thus be addressed mostly to those who act as pastors and Bible teachers (and to those who are training for such ministry). However, we should also acknowledge (while we are laying down our definitions) that the sermon in the Sunday gathering is by no means the only context in which sermons are preached.

Sermons are delivered at funerals and weddings, at graduations and on special occasions, at evangelistic rallies and conferences, at men's breakfasts and women's coffee mornings and youth rallies and kids' clubs. There are many contexts in which sermons are preached, and these different situations will affect the relationship between preacher and audience, and the nature of the communication. However, the heart and aim of all of them is the same—to declare God's word truthfully and faithfully.

Why we fail

Despite the fact that it has become trendy these days to claim the name 'evangelical', and to espouse undying love for 'expository preaching', the practice in many pulpits on any given Sunday suggests that our outspoken desire to expound God's word is not always translated into reality. Why does this happen?

It is impossible to cite all of the permutations of human sinfulness involved, but let us try to outline some of the forces that keep us from preaching the pure word of God.

Perhaps our first problem is encapsulated in that dreadful word 'relevance'. In a world where the consumer knows best, there is no greater crime than 'irrelevance'. As is regularly pointed out, if no-one is listening, it doesn't matter what you're saying. And it's a critique that is keenly felt by many pastors.

These days, churches compete with sport, shopping, socializing, entertainment and even slothfulness for attention —apparently many people prefer to sleep in on Sunday mornings! And so we feel the pressure to be relevant, the pressure to see more people walking in through our doors—a pressure that is amplified and confused by our mixed motives. At one level, we just want to see people won for Christ. But our pride also longs for others to notice the 'success' of our ministry and ask our advice, and our self-protectiveness knows that the management committee is constantly watching the bottom line. For any number of reasons, most pastors today experience an intense pressure to see more people coming through the door.

Moreover, in our 'always on' world, increasingly controlled by social media and constant connection, we are told that we must listen to the consumer or die. The fundamental doctrines of the new millennium are freedom and autonomy; choice is king. We are constantly encouraged to ask: What do people in our world want from church? What are the topics that they want us to talk about? What will interest people in coming to visit us? With the best of intentions, we are left with the democracy of sinful souls as the arbiter of our message. For without doubt, the words of God about sin and judgement are not the words that seem guaranteed to attract more people to listen.

Hand in hand with this emphasis on autonomy and freedom has come the importance of listening. To be relevant, we must engage the world outside the walls of the church in 'conversation'. In one sense, this is what we should have always been doing—talking to people who don't know Christ about the love and mercy of God. But the problem lies in what we mean by 'conversation'.

'Conversation' has come to mean accepting all opinions as equally valid. To declare that I am right and that you are wrong is the social equivalent of bathing in manure. The direct result is a growing discomfort about preaching the truths of God as the truths of God. Rather than announcing "this is what God says", we gradually water down the message to make it more acceptable. We pick up the Bible and ask what Jesus might contribute to the conversation. The effect is to reduce God to our level. God does not declare or demand—he suggests. And we begin to read his word as a human document with hints of the divine. Tucked away in the bottom drawer of our systematic theology is the belief that the Bible is still God's word, but unspoken beliefs are quickly forgotten.

As part of the process, we buy into the atomization of the Bible. We preach about 'what Paul says' or 'what Peter thinks'. It is not wrong to notice that Paul uses a different vocabulary from Peter; nor should we shy away from the fact that Isaiah possessed a different personality from Jeremiah. Miraculously, Scripture is God's word through human authors. But does our preaching remind our hearers that they are listening to a word from the living God? Do we remind our congregation that this word has one divine author who stands behind and speaks through the entire biblical word, from Genesis to Revelation?

Slowly but surely, our confidence in the word of God has been undermined. In our desire to be part of the 'conversation', we long for the acceptance and legitimacy that will never come. And our preaching starts to be sprinkled with phrases like 'the way I see it' and 'it seems to me'.

At first glance, introducing our ideas with 'I think' rather than declaring 'God says' conveys a wise and thoughtful humility. We acknowledge that we aren't gurus to whom people should come for answers. We invite the outsider and the sceptic to come and listen. But ultimately the appearance of humility cloaks the anxiety of an unbelieving heart. Why should people come and listen to what we think, when there are so many wiser and more capable people in the world to listen to? Surely the reason we have anything to say at all is that we do not speak our own wisdom but the wisdom that comes from above.

True humility is to speak the words of God. False humility is to speak our own words as if our words are what matter. People shouldn't come to hear the preacher. People should come to hear God.

What if God showed up this Sunday?

If God guaranteed you that he would visit your church this Sunday, and bring a message to the congregation, direct from his own lips, speaking his life-changing truth to the spiritual needs of all, would you think about cutting one or two songs, and giving God some extra time? Would you ask the drama team to postpone their 20-minute re-enactment of the Prodigal Son? Would you feel the need, if you were the minister, to put aside some time after God had spoken to tell some stories that made the divine message a bit more real and relevant to the people?

If God did turn up in all his blazing glory to deliver a message to your church, what would your reaction be? Hopefully you would scrap everything, fall trembling on your knees, and say, "Speak, Lord, your servants are listening".

The truth is, of course, that God is with us whenever we gather, and he speaks his very words to us. Whenever we open God's Scriptures and read his words, he is with us and he speaks. And yet by our actions—by the way we run our meetings, and by the way we preach—we often demonstrate that we don't really believe in the transforming power of his words.

This is what speaking the oracles of God means: it means saying what God would say if he were to turn up at your church. It means saying what God did say when he was here on earth in the person of his Son. It means saying what God has said, and continues to say, through the inspired Scriptures. True preaching is preaching that unfolds and explicates and explains and declares the living and active words of God.

Without this conviction everything else in this book is meaningless. It is the foundation of every faithful preacher's preaching.

Chapter 2

My aim is to preach the gospel

Cricket is a peculiarly British game that can end in a draw after five days of play—a sum total of 30 hours of game time. Perhaps even more bizarrely, most people who love the game are able to conceive of this as a good result. It's the kind of game that you either love or hate (to your own detriment). For cricket-lovers, you really haven't lived until you've sat through the last two hours of an intensely fought draw on the edge of your seat!

However, our aim here is not to extol the glories of cricket but rather to use it as an illustration. The length and complexity of the game mean that it is mastered over years rather than minutes or days. There may be a moment when a young boy decides he wants to play cricket—a moment when he is captured by the game and begins to harbour the desire to one day play for his country. But that moment isn't all that is required to produce a cricketer. It is a necessary moment, but not a sufficient moment. The same is true of becoming a preacher.

Many of us have been challenged and convicted in the past to preach the very words of God. And in chapter 1, we highlighted the vital importance of preaching only what God wants to say to his people. But it is one thing to feel that conviction; it is another to put it into practice.

What will it look like to speak the oracles of God? Let's begin by looking at a sentence that has been 40 years in the making. We might call it the preacher's mission statement:

> *My aim is to preach the gospel by prayerfully expounding the Bible to the people God has given me to love.*

The words are carefully chosen and each part of the statement is worth pondering. We will return to the final phrase in due course, but we would do well to begin by remembering that pastors don't preach to the church they create but to the congregation that God gathers and places under their care. The people in our ministry are God's and not ours. The goal of ministry isn't to grow our personal kingdom but God's kingdom, and the pastor's job is not primarily to rule the church, but to love God's people—to love them by preaching the gospel through prayerful Bible exposition.

Yet while the whole statement is worth reflecting on, it is probably the idea of 'preaching the gospel by prayerfully expounding the Bible' that needs the most explanation. If, as we have suggested, the primary aim of the preacher is to say what God says, wouldn't 'prayerfully expounding the Bible' be enough to fulfil that goal? Why add the aim of 'preaching the gospel'? And how is preaching the gospel related to prayerful exposition of the Bible?

What is the gospel?

'Gospel' is the king of evangelical words because the 'evangel' is the 'gospel'. We have chosen to call ourselves evangelicals because we want to be gospel people. And we want to be gospel people because, since the time Christ walked on earth, God's people have been gospel people. The apostles were gospel people; they summarized their whole ministry in terms of the gospel. Paul was set aside for the gospel of God (Rom 1:1), and his life's mission was to make the gospel known to all nations (Rom 15:14-21). The gospel is God's message for the world, and neither humans nor angels have the authority to change it (Galatians 1-2).

But our problem is that 'gospel' is such an all-encompassing word that it's sometimes hard to know what we mean by it. Think for a moment about the different ways that evangelicals commonly use the word 'gospel', and how that might affect our mission statement above. Sometimes the gospel is evangelical shorthand for justification by faith alone. But if that is all we mean by gospel then our preaching mission statement becomes an encouragement to preach justification by faith alone every time we open the Bible. As important a doctrine as it is, is justification by faith alone the summary of *everything* we should preach? Or what if we think of the gospel as the events of Jesus' life, especially his death and resurrection? Are we to preach the life, death and resurrection of Jesus from every passage in the Bible? And if so, how would we do that?

While it can feel tedious to do so—don't we all know the gospel, weren't we all saved by hearing it?—it is worth stopping for a moment to reflect on what we mean by the gospel. Or rather, what God means by the gospel.

The gospel of the kingdom of God

In the New Testament, our first encounter with the word *euangelion* (the Greek word for 'gospel') comes, unsurprisingly, in the Gospels. And perhaps most famously, in the introduction to Mark's history of Jesus: "The beginning of the *gospel* of Jesus Christ, the Son of God" (Mark 1:1). We are used to the idea that the gospel means 'good news' or perhaps more accurately just 'news'.[1] Mark wants us to know that his Gospel contains the news about Jesus Christ, the Son of God. As the Gospel unfolds we meet and hear and come to understand this Jesus. What is the gospel in this verse? It is the recounting of the life, teaching, death and resurrection of Jesus.

But we don't get far before a fly hops into the ointment. If the gospel is the account of Jesus' life, teaching, death and resurrection, then what on earth was Jesus preaching?

> Now after John was arrested, Jesus came into Galilee, proclaiming the gospel of God, and saying, "The time is fulfilled, and the kingdom of God is at hand; repent and believe in the gospel". (Mark 1:14-15)

What was the gospel that Jesus preached? Did he come and detail all the events of his life and explain the significance of his death and resurrection from the outset of his ministry?

Clearly not. If Jesus had been preaching his death from the beginning then it would not have come as such a shock when Jesus explained to his disciples that his mission in life was to die (Mark 8:31ff). Peter responds to Jesus' words in Mark 8 as someone hearing them for the first time—someone who hears but doesn't understand.

Jesus didn't come preaching his own death from the very beginning; he came preaching what Mark records for us: the kingdom of God is at hand; now is the time to repent and believe the announcement. When the word 'gospel' is replaced by this somewhat more mundane word 'announcement', we get some of the sense of what Jesus was saying. To paraphrase

---

1. Broughton Knox argues (persuasively) that the word 'gospel', as such, simply means 'news'. It is the context and nature of the announcement that determine whether it is good news for those who hear it. See 'Meaning of the word "gospel"' in T Payne and K Beilharz (eds), *D. Broughton Knox: Selected Works*, vol. III, Matthias Media, Sydney, 2006, pp. 59-60.

Mark 1:14-15: the kingdom of God is at hand, turn to God and believe the announcement I am making to you.

But in Mark's account, even the early events of Jesus' ministry, when read through Old Testament glasses, give a clear insight into what Jesus meant when he declared that the kingdom was at hand. According to Mark 1, Jesus came preaching in order to fulfil the prophecy of John the Baptist, who himself came in fulfilment of Isaiah's prophecy (in chapter 40). To understand what Jesus meant when he preached the coming of the kingdom, we must first understand Isaiah.

The first half of Isaiah is an indictment on Israel for their constant rebellion against God. God promises that he will judge his people by sending them into captivity in a foreign land. But this is not his final word. Isaiah 40 contains the promise that this terrible judgement isn't the end for God's people. A time will come when God himself will tread down the mountains and raise up the valleys and create a highway from Babylon to Jerusalem. God will come and rescue his people. And in the time before God comes to restore his people, a voice will cry out in the desert, calling upon people to prepare themselves for God's arrival.

John the Baptist is this voice calling on people to be ready for God to come to bring an end to the exile. But as impressive as John's ministry and call to repentance may have been—and we know it was impressive enough to bring the masses out into the wilderness to be baptized in the Jordan—anyone listening carefully would have known that he wasn't the main act. John kept saying, watch for the one coming after me—"After me comes he who is mightier than I, the strap of whose sandals I am not worthy to stoop down and untie. I have baptized you with water, but he will baptize you with the Holy Spirit" (Mark 1:7-8).

Just as it would be foolish to go to Niagara Falls in order to see the sign that says 'Niagara Falls' without looking at the actual falls, so it would be foolish to see John and then fail to look for the one he is pointing to. The big news isn't that John is here but that John has come to prepare the way. He is the curtain-raiser to the main act, the signpost to the reality. So who is the reality? Jesus steps straight onto the scene and is baptized, not just with water, but with the Spirit of God. And the Father himself confirms Jesus' identity.

Jesus is God's "beloved Son", the one with whom he is "well pleased". Perhaps surprisingly for us, God is quoting himself. His words here about Jesus are a combination of two words that he spoke in the Old Testament: one from Psalm 2:7 and the other from Isaiah 42:1. The Psalm 2 reference reminds us of God's promise to install his Son in Zion as the eternal king who will judge every ruler on the earth. But the Isaiah reference is strange. It is about the servant, the meek one who will not snuff out a burning wick, and who will bring forth justice to the nations, and who (as Isaiah says a few chapters later) will die for the sins of his people (Isaiah 53).

Those who stood and watched John baptize Jesus may not have understood what they were seeing, but the signs were there for those with the eyes to see. God's Old Testament promises were being fulfilled. Jesus had come as the promised Christ and as the suffering servant.

But Jesus didn't preach the gospel by proclaiming all of these details. He simply told the people that God was finally fulfilling the promises of the prophets, that the kingdom had arrived, and that now was the time to repent. It's not that his death and resurrection were irrelevant. Indeed, the very fact that he was the Christ meant, by definition, that he had come to lay down his life for his people (Mark 8:27-9:1). More than that, because he entered this world as God's king, the grave could not contain him—he had to rise again on the third day (Mark 8:31, 9:31, 10:34). You cannot separate the Christ from the Old Testament promises of suffering and vindication.

Nevertheless, Jesus could preach that he was the king bringing the kingdom without all of the details. What mattered was that God was bringing in his kingdom and that now was the time to respond to what God was doing. But here is the key. What Jesus preached in embryo beside the Jordan River, the apostles preached in all of its fullness to whomever would listen. Kingdom preaching is gospel preaching and gospel preaching is kingdom preaching. Jesus preached the gospel of the kingdom (Matt 4:23, 9:35), then promised that the gospel of the kingdom would be preached in all the world (Matt 24:14), and then the apostles went about preaching the kingdom (Acts 8:12; 14:22; 19:8; 20:25; 28:23, 31).

For the apostles, preaching the gospel of the kingdom meant telling everyone they could find that Jesus had died and been raised as God's true king, and therefore it was time to repent and turn to him. This is the constant pattern of the apostolic sermons in Acts. While each of the sermons contains its own nuances, the repeated elements paint a very clear picture. Jesus was descended from David (Acts 2:30, 13:22-23), put to death on a cross (Acts 2:23, 10:39, 13:28-29), and raised from the dead in fulfilment of God's promises as the Christ (Acts 2:24-36, 3:15, 10:40-42, 13:32-39). Therefore now is the time to seek his forgiveness through repentance and faith (Acts 2:38, 3:19-20, 10:43, 13:39), for the judgement is coming (Acts 10:42, 17:31).

Jesus preached the gospel and he sent the apostles out preaching the same gospel. But preaching the gospel didn't mean explaining every last detail of his death and resurrection every time they preached. Nor did it mean saying exactly the same thing every time they spoke. The message about God's fulfilment of his kingdom, through the death and resurrection of Jesus, was preached wisely and thoughtfully in each new situation.

What is the gospel? It has been suggested that 'gospel' is a portmanteau word—which may not help if you don't know what a portmanteau is (it's a carpetbag or suitcase that expands as you add to its contents). What this means is that the gospel is as simple as 'Jesus is Lord'. But telling someone that "Jesus is the Lord who died for sins" is also telling the gospel. And proclaiming "Jesus is the Lord who died for sins and has been raised as the head of a new humanity who commands all people to repent and turn to him as the judge of the living and the dead" is also preaching the gospel.

What does all of this mean for the biblical preacher?

The gospel circle

The key is found in understanding the relationship between the gospel and the entire biblical revelation. As we've just seen briefly, the gospel—the message about Jesus—is the centre and the fulfilment of the whole of God's revelation. God spoke many things at many times and in many ways through the prophets, but in these last days, in the final phase of his plans for the world, he has spoken in his Son, who is the beginning and the end, the one through whom he created the world, and the one who will inherit all things (Heb 1:1-2).

To put it another way, the Old Testament is an unfinished book. It is not the 'Hebrew Scriptures' (as it is trendy to call it these days), but the Christian Scriptures, written for our instruction "on whom the end of the ages has come" (1 Cor 10:11). The Old Testament is the prologue and introduction and scene-setting for God's final revelation in Christ. As the author to the Hebrews puts it at the end of his catalogue of the heroes of Old Testament faith:

> And all these, though commended through their faith, did not receive what was promised, since God had provided something better for us, that apart from us they should not be made perfect. (Heb 11:39-40)

Jesus himself taught that he was the key to understanding the Old Testament Scriptures:

> Then he said to them, "These are my words that I spoke to you while I was still with you, that everything written about me in the Law of Moses and the Prophets and the Psalms must be fulfilled." Then he opened their minds to understand the Scriptures, and said to them, "Thus it is written, that the Christ should suffer and on the third day rise from the dead, and that repentance and forgiveness of sins should be proclaimed in his name to all nations, beginning from Jerusalem." (Luke 24:44-47)

And he rebuked the Pharisees for failing to see this:

> "You search the Scriptures because you think that in them you have eternal life; and it is they that bear witness about me, yet you refuse to come to me that you may have life." (John 5:39-40)

The gospel is the key that unlocks the message of the whole Bible. In short, the gospel of Christ is the message that we must preach from the Scriptures because it is the message that the Scriptures preach.

However, when we think about the gospel as the 'key' or the 'centre' of the biblical revelation, we most naturally conceive of the centre as a point. After all, the centre of a circle is the dot in the middle. But the gospel is much more than the dot in the centre of the Bible. The gospel is much better envisaged as a circle that encompasses the whole of the Bible's message.

Why should we envisage it as a circle? Most importantly because it reminds us of the portmanteau nature of the gospel. The gospel is not one simple little truth contained at the heart of the Bible, but a rich and complex truth. Were you to examine the gospel circle closely, you would see that the circumference of the circle is made up of many different arcs—arcs of varying length and significance, but all of which are necessary for articulating the truth of the Bible.

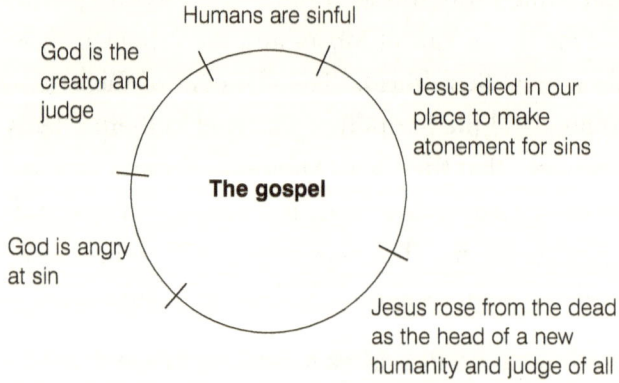

Now this is not meant to be an exhaustive diagram, but the point is clear enough. At the heart of biblical truth is the message about God's relationship with his creation, the devastating reality of human sinfulness, and the gracious love of God that gives up his Son for the restoration of the universe under God's faithful rule. To truly understand what it means for Jesus to be Lord we must bring together many biblical truths in the way that the Bible brings them together.

By remembering the gospel circle that encompasses the message of the Bible, the preacher is constantly reminded to preach the Scriptures in light of what God wants us to hear in the Scriptures. We are also reminded that the gospel is not simplistic. Inevitably, each passage we preach will touch upon some parts of the circle but not necessarily all of the circle. We are not called upon to preach the entire circumference each and every week. Rather, we are called upon to preach the arcs of the gospel that God puts in front of us in the passage.

But the flipside is also true. For any true circle, one arc of the circle implies the whole. So by remembering that each passage we preach is an arc of the circle, we encourage ourselves to preach it in a way that fits in with the whole gospel message. We should never preach a particular passage in such a way that people are going to end up with an oval or a pear or even a square when they hear from another part of God's word next week.

But there is another vitally important thing that understanding the gospel circle achieves. It reminds us over and over again that the Bible is to be *preached*. At the heart of the Scriptures is not a treatise or a learned work but the message of life and death. It is not a message to be lectured or simply taught or mined for interesting information. It is a message to be preached.

The apostles understood that the end of the ages was upon them and that the judgement was just around the corner (Acts 17:30-31). And so they didn't rise up on Sunday morning to explain that there were interesting perspectives in this word that you might choose to adopt if they happened to fit in with your faith journey. They didn't canvas the various options and perspectives that might shed light on what this word actually meant. And they didn't provide a verbal commentary, detailing some of the idiosyncrasies of biblical Hebrew. They preached that God's king had come and that today was the day to repent.

By saying that our aim is to preach the gospel, we remind ourselves over and over again that the Bible has a pointy end. God hasn't given us his word to entertain us, enthral us, enrich us and certainly not just to inform us. It will do all of those things, but none of them are God's primary purpose in giving us his precious word. God has given his word so that we might be reborn to new life by responding, through the work of the Spirit, to God's call to repent and trust his Son. Because it is impossible to preach the gospel without calling on people to respond, it is impossible to preach any part of God's word without calling on people to obey it.

Today if you hear his voice

In order to see this more clearly, let's turn to Hebrews 3 and 4, where the writer shows us so plainly that the Spirit still speaks God's word today as the Scriptures are read. The call of these chapters is to enter God's eternal rest by trusting in Jesus, our great high priest, who sympathizes with our weakness and who has passed through the heavens on our behalf. In order to call us to trust in Christ, the author of Hebrews uses the words of Psalm 95.

The fascinating thing about Psalm 95 is that it in turn speaks of the events that occurred at Massah and Meribah as Israel wandered in the wilderness—those places of rebellion where the people refused to listen to God, and God judged their disobedience. Psalm 95 is the call to those living in David's day to listen to God—"Today if you hear his voice, do not harden your hearts" (vv. 7-8). But the call to listen and repent as you hear "today" is the call to learn from what had happened hundreds of years before in Israel's history.

According to Hebrews, the Holy Spirit who spoke that word of warning in David's day is still speaking the same word of warning as Psalm 95 is read today. Psalm 95 is not some archaic word that might help you to live a better life, but the word of God, which God is still speaking 'today' and every day that the Psalm is read. Psalm 95 is not a museum piece; it is the active, powerful word of God calling people to repentance and faith.

That is why, in the Anglican *Book of Common Prayer*, Psalm 95 is required reading every time people gather for morning prayer—which when the prayer book was first produced was every day of the week. For hundreds of years, Anglicans around the world awoke every morning to speak Psalm 95 to one another before they read from the rest of the Bible. Why? As they read Psalm 95 to one another, God reminded them of the seriousness of listening to his word.

God's word is the active and powerful word of the Lord of heaven and earth. It is the sharp two-edged sword of our saviour and redeemer (Heb 4:12). And so whenever we read the Bible, the message is the same—as you listen to God's voice today, do not harden your hearts but obey.

But as we read Hebrews, we see that the word that God speaks, which we must listen to, is the word about his Son. It is the final word for the last days; the declaration of the great salvation without which there is nothing but judgement; the perfect word about the great high priest who has performed the final sacrifice and now sits at the right hand of the Father in glory.

Won't our preaching get boring?

But perhaps you feel some reservations about preaching the gospel by prayerfully expounding the Bible. Isn't it a bit reductionistic? Won't it get boring? Won't every sermon sound the same when it ends up being about how Jesus died and rose again to forgive us our sins? Isn't there more in the Bible than that?

We need to remember the gospel circle illustration and the portmanteau nature of the gospel. The biblical gospel is not exhausted or explained in all of its fullness by *The Four Spiritual Laws*, *The Bridge to Life* or even by *Two Ways to Live*. There are many arcs on the circumference of the gospel circle, and each of them is revealed and explained in multiple ways in many different parts of the Bible. Preaching the gospel by prayerfully expounding the Bible is not about overlaying every passage with your favourite gospel outline, but rather seeing how the gospel illuminates each passage that we preach and how the passage itself illuminates the gospel.

This is a key reason for shaping our preaching program around the regular exposition of different books of the Bible.

By choosing to preach from Proverbs and then Colossians and then Deuteronomy and then Luke, we keep forcing ourselves to preach the gospel in all of its richness and fullness.

Please note, the portmanteau nature of the gospel doesn't result in everything becoming the gospel. The gospel doesn't expand to encompass all of the Bible as if, somehow, "A bribe is like a magic stone in the eyes of the one who gives it; wherever he turns he prospers" (Prov 17:8) is the gospel. But every part of the Bible will relate to the gospel and ought to be preached in the light of it.

What does that mean for our proverb about bribery? We need to read it in the context of the rest of the Bible, and in particular, the context of the gospel. The book of Proverbs is full of wisdom, garnered by observing the world in light of the knowledge of God—it is the fear of the Lord that is the beginning of wisdom. In other words, we understand God's world rightly as we observe it as his creation. This wisdom makes sense as we fear God—as we know and trust the creator and judge of the world who is fully and finally revealed in Jesus as three-in-one. Therefore, the wisdom of Proverbs only finally makes sense in light of God's kingdom established in the death and resurrection of his Christ.

The rest of the Bible, with Christ's coming at its centre, helps us to see that Proverbs 17:8 is not an encouragement to take up bribery as a way of life, but an observation about how good bribery looks to the one who uses it to make their way in the world. But as we read the New Testament and see that Jesus' people keep in step with the Spirit of Christ by speaking honestly and rejecting falsehood, we understand how to read the proverb rightly. The book of Proverbs observes God's world and sets out what it means to live well in it, in light of the fear of the creator. That way of life is fulfilled and completed by Christ's coming. Therefore we read Proverbs as Christians, in the light of the coming of Jesus.

Our understanding of the gospel supplies the categories through which we read and understand the whole Bible, including the Old Testament. The lordship of the creator, the sinfulness of humanity and our need of forgiveness, the doctrine of the resurrection of the dead and God's revelation of his plans for creation—all of these should shape and mould our reading of the Bible. And so we should seek to preach the Bible in such a way as to call people to live under the lordship of Christ, through whom God offers forgiveness, life and hope.

But this further explains why our gospel preaching should never be boring. 'Jesus is Lord' is not some platonic ideal that never actually touches the real world. It is his sovereign rule over the lives of his people. As we speak about the Lord who has given his life for us and been raised as our king, we must point out, just as the Bible does, what this means for the whole of our lives.

Christ's lordship will affect everything from our understanding of how we are made right with God (Rom 5:1-11) to the way we treat the outsider among us (Jas 2:1-9), from our appreciation of God's mercy (Rom 11:33-12:1) to what we do with our sexuality (1 Cor 6:12-20), from the fruit of our lips (Jas 3:10; cf. Heb 13:15) to where, how and when we spend our money (2 Corinthians 8-9). Christ's lordship is not some abstract principle, but a concrete reality. And we respond to his lordship in small and large ways every day, from accepting that he alone is able to deal with our sins (Acts 4:12) to disciplining our children with wisdom and care (Eph 6:4). All these aspects—whether the doctrinal content of our faith or the details of the Christian life—are elements of understanding and responding to the lordship of Christ.

Most importantly of all, our understanding of the lordship of Christ is tied directly to his coronation as king through his death in our place and resurrection to new life.

The benefits of preaching the gospel

Let's pause and recap. What have we seen in this chapter? The gospel, the message about Jesus' life, death and resurrection, is the central message of the Bible. It is the message that God is seeking to communicate in all of his word. And so we preach the Bible rightly as we seek to *preach the gospel* by prayerfully expounding God's word.

Beginning with the desire to preach the gospel reminds us to preach the Bible as the word of God—the word that calls on everyone who hears, every time they hear it, to respond with obedience and faith. We must not preach the Bible without calling on people to respond to it. Further, by aiming to preach the gospel we remind ourselves to preach the whole of the Scriptures with reference to Christ, the point and purpose of all of God's work in the world. In short, by aiming to preach the gospel, we remind ourselves to preach the oracles of God as the oracles of God.

Chapter 3

Preaching the gospel by expounding the Bible

So far, we've established that true preaching involves speaking the words of God, as the words of God, to whomever will listen. And in the last chapter we saw that having the goal of preaching the gospel as we teach the Bible is a vital element of any preaching ministry because the gospel is at the heart of the biblical revelation. The next logical step involves understanding how to preach the gospel *by prayerfully expounding the Bible.*

Prayerfully

Before we look at what 'expounding the Bible' means (and we will do so in depth), we should linger over that easily overlooked word, 'prayerfully'.

All preaching must be prayerful, because no preaching is effective unless God is at work in it. We can plant and water as much as we like, but without God there will be no growth (1 Cor 3:6). Indeed, without the powerful work of God's Spirit within, there will be no understanding of the passage by the preacher, and no understanding and conviction within those who hear. We need God to be at work at every point in the process, and so we need to be in prayer at every point in the process.

We should pray and seek God's wisdom as we prepare to preach, begging him to remove our blindness and to help us see new treasures in his word. We should pray that God would bring people to the meeting and prepare their hearts for the message. We should pray as we walk to the pulpit that God would calm our nerves and guard our lips, so that we would speak the truth in love. We should pray as we begin the sermon, not only to signal the supernatural nature of what we are doing, but also to ask God to speak to all of us and to move our hearts to repentance and faith. We should pray at the conclusion of the sermon, summarizing the main thing that God is saying to us, and asking him to change our hearts and minds by his Spirit. We should pray afterwards as a congregation in response to what God has said—whether in thanksgiving or confession or petition. And we should pray in the days following the sermon that God would write the words we have heard into our hearts, and incline us to obey them day by day.

All of this is easy to understand, and impossible to argue with. We know that we need God to be at work in every aspect of preaching—both in the preacher and the hearers. We know equally that he responds to and uses our prayers in his powerful work. And yet we so easily and frequently neglect to pray. We can preach competently, earnestly, faithfully, intelligently, interestingly, missionally, passionately, humorously and even brilliantly. But we fail when we do not preach *prayerfully*.

Expounding the Bible

What, then, does it mean to expound the Bible? With the growing popularity of evangelicalism, 'expository' preaching become quite the fashion. Everyone seems to be interested in expounding the Bible these days. Unfortunately, this has resulted not so much in an explosion of faithful biblical preaching as a devaluing of the currency. Words like 'expound' (and its adjective 'expository') have been so widely applied to such a variety of preaching that it's hard to know what they mean any more.

This is a shame, because 'expound' is a good word to describe what preachers do when they speak the oracles of God. To expound is to "set forth or state in detail" according to the *Macquarie Dictionary*. It is to start with an existing text or message, and to explain it, elaborate upon it, and argue for it. It is what the Levites did for the people in Nehemiah 8:8: "They read from the book, from the Law of God, clearly, and they gave the sense, so that the people understood the reading".

This is also what Jesus did for the two baffled disciples on the road to Emmaus in Luke 24. Beginning with Moses and all the Prophets, he explained to them "in all the Scriptures the things concerning himself" (Luke 24:27).[2] Later in the same chapter, he does something similar for the assembled disciples: "Then he opened their minds to understand the Scriptures, and said to them, 'Thus it is written, that the Christ should suffer and on the third day rise from the dead, and that repentance and forgiveness of sins should be proclaimed in his name to all nations, beginning from Jerusalem'" (Luke 24:45-47). Interestingly, the same word for 'open up' is translated as 'explain' to describe Paul's activity in Acts 17:

> And Paul went in, as was his custom, and on three Sabbath days he reasoned with them from the Scriptures, *explaining* and proving that it was necessary for the Christ to suffer and to rise from the dead, and saying, "This Jesus, whom I proclaim to you, is the Christ". (Acts 17:2-3)

---

2. The NIV has "explained". The ESV, less happily in our view, uses "interpreted".

Philip's interaction with the Ethiopian eunuch in Acts 8 provides another example of the same kind of explaining or exposition of the biblical text. Philip asks the eunuch whether he understands the Scripture that he is reading, and when the eunuch asks for a guide, Philip jumps up into the chariot and evangelizes him, starting with Isaiah 53.

We may need a better word than 'expound' to capture what is happening in these examples, but for the moment we're using 'expound' to talk about how someone starts with the Scripture and then explains it, opens up its meaning, and uses it to 'prove' the truth about God and Christ and the gospel.

Let us look further at what we mean by 'expounding' the Bible.

Firstly, genuine expository preaching will respect the nature of the whole Bible as the word of God. What does that look like in practice?

It means planning to preach the whole of the Bible rather than just the parts that we find enjoyable or comfortable. This doesn't necessarily mean having a plan to preach every single chapter of the Bible in a certain period of time, but if our goal is to preach the whole Bible then we will make decisions about what we preach and how we preach it in order to expose ourselves and our congregation to as much of the Bible as possible over time.

There are two keys to achieving this. The first is to ensure that we preach from many different parts of the Bible. For true expository preachers, this means preaching through individual books of the Bible and ensuring that the books cover the breadth and depth of the biblical revelation. Over two or three years we want people exposed to Old Testament and New Testament; to the Pentateuch, the prophets and the wisdom literature, as well as to the Gospels and the New Testament epistles.

By choosing books from all parts of the Bible, the preacher

forces himself to engage with the fullness of God's revelation and not just with those parts of the Bible that he feels most at home in. It also encourages us to listen to God on his terms, not ours; to allow God's word to set the agenda of our thinking and preaching.

But of course, it is not just enough to preach from many different books; it is also important to preach each of those books in a way that does justice to the book involved. Expository preaching is committed to working section by section through each book in a way that is sensitive to the literature. This means that sometimes you might choose to preach on several chapters at a time and sometimes on sections shorter than a chapter. But it will mean working at depth through an entire book in order that we wrestle with all that God has to say.

The main aim of this process is to ensure that we encounter God in all of his fullness, and that we hear his plans for his world in all their richness. Preaching like this will force us to deal with the Holy God who judges as well as the faithful God who keeps his word. We will meet the tender God who loves his children and rescues them in spite of their disobedience, as well as the God who rules in sovereign might and who has subjected this creation to futility so that it might yearn for a new day. A good expository preaching program will aim to work through books from the whole breadth of the canon, from Genesis to Revelation. That is a key part of what we mean by prayerfully expounding the Bible.

But perhaps the hardest part of this task is sitting down, week by week, with a section of Scripture and seeking to understand and communicate it. The next few chapters are about how someone moves from reading a section of Scripture to preparing a talk that faithfully 'sets forth and states in detail' God's truths contained in that part of the Bible. How does 'expository' preaching move from the text to the sermon?

In order to explain that process, we're going to use an illustration that revolves around the ancient practice of archery. Now like all illustrations, this one is imperfect and does not pertain at every point (as will become clear as we 'expound' it). And let us warn you in advance not to take the illustration and run too far with it, and find yourself having left both the Bible and good sense behind.

However, we want to suggest that preaching is like archery, and sermon preparation is like fletching (the process of making arrows). An archer's job is to deliver the arrowhead deep into the heart of his target. In order to do the job well, the right arrows are required. Some arrows fly further but are less accurate. Some arrows are better for piercing armour but more expensive to produce. Different arrows are required to do different jobs.

The preacher's job is to fletch the appropriate arrows (sermons) and then fire (preach) them well. But in order to understand the illustration you need to know something about arrows. Arrows have three essential components—an arrowhead, a shaft and the feathers.

The three essential parts of the arrow

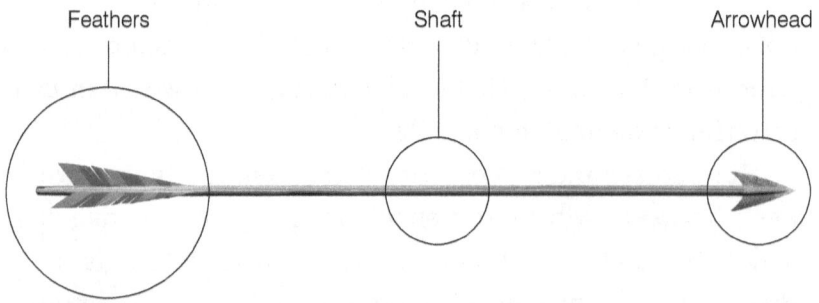

The arrowhead is the part of the arrow that does the damage. It pierces the target and cuts to the heart. The last chapter was effectively about the arrowhead of the sermon. At the point of the arrowhead is the gospel, the declaration that Jesus is the Lord and Saviour. The cutting edges of the arrowhead are the implications of that reality. This can include things like ethics, philosophy, apologetics, personal godliness and *kategoria*.[3]

The kind of head that you fit to your arrow should be governed primarily by the text being preached, but also secondarily by the context of the sermon. Our regular week-by-week Sunday sermons should simply be driven by the text for that day, but in other circumstances (weddings, funerals, and so on), the demands and purposes of the occasion will affect the text chosen and the nature of the arrowhead.

However, it is worth emphasizing at this point that unlike any other sort of meeting, when we gather as a church our purpose is to hear the word of God. On the archetypal 'day of the assembly', when the people of Israel 'churched' around God at Mount Sinai, the Lord's purpose was "that I may let them hear my words" (Deut 4:10; cf. 9:10, 10:4). Likewise, when the great assembly gathers around the Son in the heavenly Jerusalem in Hebrews, they hear the better word of Jesus' blood (Heb 12:24).

Whatever else we may do when we come together—to give thanks to him, to make melody in our hearts to him, to cast our cares upon him—we primarily gather to "hear his most holy word" (as *The Book of Common Prayer* puts it). Ultimately, the preacher has no other agenda or goal but to make God's word clear to the church. There may be occasions of preaching where this is not the case—such as at a school prize-giving. In these

---

3. *Kategoria* is the opposite of *apologia* (apologetics). If apologetics is answering the questions that the world asks of the gospel, then *kategoria* is pointing out the questions that the gospel asks of the world.

circumstances we may still be able to preach God's word, but it is not the primary purpose or function of the gathering. But in the gathering of God's people that we call 'church', making God's word known is the primary purpose.

The purest preaching happens in the context where God's servant is preaching God's word to God's people. This makes both church going and church preaching critical. In our gatherings, we must be careful not to allow other elements to crowd out the hearing of God's word. It happens easily enough. Sometimes it's singing; sometimes it's long interviews and announcements and news about what is happening in the church's program; sometimes it's simply an overly short meeting, with the aim of getting people in and out before they get bored. But however it happens, when the hearing of God's word is reduced to one short Bible reading and a quick sermon, we have lost touch with why we are getting together in church in the first place.

It is just as critical that what is preached is put into action within the gathering. For example, to preach the priesthood and ministry of all believers but to run our meetings as if the pastoral staff are the only ones allowed to say or do anything is really to make a nonsense of what is being preached. Likewise, we can't preach 1 Timothy 2 and 1 Corinthians 14 without implementing what those passages say about the role of male elders and pastors in preaching in the congregational gathering. In other contexts, such as a women's Bible study, women may well preach, but God's word says that women are not to teach and have authority over men.

Faithful preaching will continually challenge the church to reform, to examine and re-examine its life and practices and habits in the light of God's word. But of course, this sort of preaching risks conflict, because that is what usually happens when the status quo is challenged. And so we naturally shy away from preaching the contentious topics and the contentious passages. This is faithless. The preacher's task is to preach God's words, not to decide which of God's words might be most palatable or cause the least fuss. We must not give in to pressure from congregation members to avoid certain topics or to soft-pedal the truth. We must also never undermine the integrity of the pulpit by inviting people to preach for political reasons—because it will appease certain members or because it will advance our standing in some way. The reason any person stands up to preach is to proclaim the words of God—to plant the arrowhead of the gospel into the hearts of his hearers.

One of the keys to shaping good arrowheads is to notice whether there are any imperatives (or commands) given by the writer in the passage. The application of the truths in the passage may well be broader than these particular imperatives, but they will never be less. And if we pay particular attention to the commands given in the passage it will help us focus on what God wants us to do rather than on our own particular prejudices.

An example of this occurs in 1 Corinthians 12. There is only one imperative in this chapter—in the final verse.[4] After Paul has explained that the Spirit's primary work is to lead people to call on Christ as their Lord (1 Cor 12:3), that God—Father, Son and Holy Spirit—has given gifts to his body for the common good (1 Cor 12:4-11), and that the body is one body in Christ that needs every member (1 Cor 12:12-30), he then commands his readers to earnestly desire the greater gifts (1 Cor 12:31). Furthermore, Paul indicates that his argument hasn't finished, because as he tells us to desire the greater gifts he also tells us that he is about to show us the more excellent way.

---

4. Indeed, even this may be an indicative rather than an imperative: "you desire" rather than "desire". For the sake of the illustration and the discussion, we will follow DA Carson and the majority in regarding it as an imperative.

The point of this whole section is not to provide a gifts inventory, nor is it to teach us about the gifts of the Spirit, for the gifts are given here by the whole Godhead. The burden of this chapter (and the following ones) is that we understand the unity of the body created by God through Christ, and thus desire those things that will build that body. Noticing the imperative in verse 31 helps us to put the emphasis in the right place, and to construct the right kind of arrowhead. It also forces us to preach 1 Corinthians 12 in light of chapters 13 and 14, and vice versa.

It is valuable to look for imperatives, but this is not to say that all arrowheads must have an imperative. When we think that no sermon is complete until it tells the congregation to *do* something, we have started to become Arminian preachers. We think that it's our job to change the congregation for the better, and that it is their job to become better Christians, and so we get into the habit of finishing every sermon with a passionate appeal for them to try harder, pray longer, obey these rules and do better.

Some Bible passages are not telling us to *do* anything, and we shouldn't be looking for something to tell people to do on the basis of these passages. It may be enough to preach the greatness of God in creation or redemption (if that is what the passage is about). It may be enough simply to open the congregation's mind to the wisdom of God, and the goodness of God, and especially the grace of God. We need to preach less about what we have to do, and more about the wonder of what God has already done for us in Christ Jesus.

We also need to be aware that sometimes there are secondary applications within a passage that are worth dwelling on. For example, in Paul's sermon in Acts 13, he says this about David: "For David, after he had served the purpose of God in his own generation, fell asleep and was laid with his fathers and saw corruption" (v. 36). Now Paul's main point in the passage is about Jesus and his death and resurrection, but on the way through he reveals a God-centred way of thinking about our lives, and the purpose of our lives, that is quite different from the way our world thinks. This is not a command to do anything, nor is it the primary point of the passage, but it provides an opportunity to challenge the world view of your congregation. Do they see their lives in terms of serving the purpose of God?

We have taken some time to talk about the arrowhead, but an arrowhead is no good on its own. You can't just fire an arrowhead; it will be hopelessly inaccurate, and even if it does hit something it won't do so with any power or direction. An arrowhead needs a shaft. The shaft corresponds to the exegesis of the passage. Just as the length and rigidity of the shaft of an arrow affects how fast, how far and how accurately an arrow will fly, so the exegesis of the passage will determine how accurately and effectively you will deliver the arrowhead of the sermon to its target. It is this question of exegesis and the formation of the shaft that we will concentrate on in the rest of this chapter.

But before we do that, let's briefly mention the feathers. An arrow that consists of only a shaft and a head will be inaccurate, and will tend to fly with sudden, random changes in direction. It will be a haphazard arrow. In order for an arrow to fly directly towards the archer's intended target, it needs to have feathers attached to the tail. For the purposes of our illustration, the feathers correspond to issues like systematic theology, biblical theology, church history, philosophy and the like. The feathers are like the big categories of thought that tie the whole message of the Bible together. We'll come to the importance of these things in the next chapter.

Here then is the finished diagram: here is what a sermon arrow looks like.

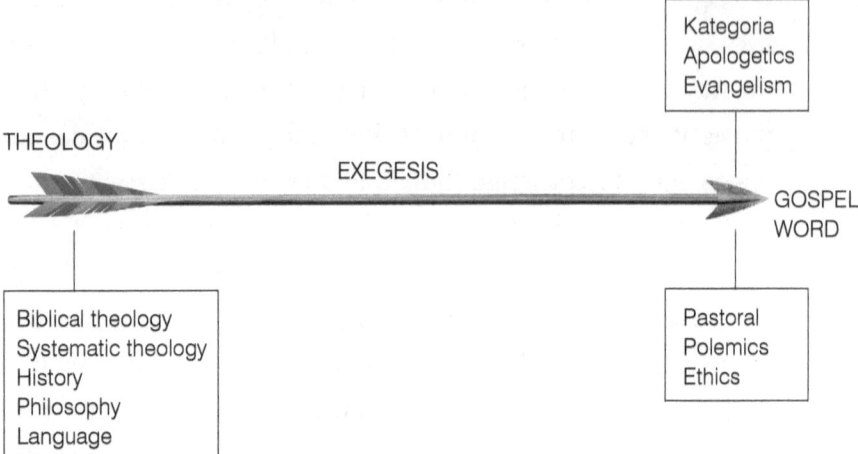

Part of the art of preaching is understanding how the passage you are teaching shapes the entire arrow. Some passages will be quite complicated to understand in their own right, and you might have to preach a sermon where you show your congregation lots of the shaft and lots of the tail feathers and it won't have a very big arrowhead. An example of this kind of passage might be Hosea 9. It is a passage full of Old Testament names and allusions. Depending on the biblical literacy of the congregation, you may need to explain who Ephraim is, or what exactly it was that happened in the days of Gibeah (Hos 9:9)—an explanation that would take you back to Judges 19. A large part of your sermon on this section of the Bible will involve just giving people the basic information they need to understand the passage.

But a sermon on Matthew 7:24-27—build your house on the rock and not the sand—involves a passage with one very straightforward main point and one main illustration. Here is an arrow that will have a very short shaft and not many tail-feathers but a great big arrowhead, as you explore with your congregation the temptations before them that could lead them to stop listening to Jesus' words.

This is a good example of the way in which an illustration fails when taken to its extreme. An arrow with a fat head, a short shaft and few feathers would fly erratically if you fired it in the real world. And the impulse to stick with the illustration might lead you to construct every sermon with the same sized head, the same length of shaft and the same number of feathers. This would be a failure to recognize the limitation of the illustration. Every sermon has a head, a shaft and feathers, but in the world of biblical preaching, you can make arrows that are perfect for the task that would never fly in the real world. The key is to fashion an arrow that does justice to the passage, because your job is to preach God's words.

We are now in a position to see more clearly why the preacher's task is to *preach the gospel by prayerfully expounding the Bible*. As we work passage by passage through different books of the Bible, our message will be shaped over time by the breadth of God's revelation rather than our own personal predispositions. If we work hard at each passage and preach it wisely, it will keep creating different kinds of arrows, with a large variety of heads and shafts and feathers. One of the great advantages of this is that it forces us to preach the whole gospel circle. Instead of being stuck preaching the gospel according to one basic gospel outline that we learned years ago, preaching the whole of Scripture ensures that we preach the gospel in all of its richness and fullness. It will also challenge us to apply the gospel in ways that we wouldn't normally think to do.

Over years of ministry, a preacher doesn't just fire one arrow but a quiver full of arrows of all sorts of different shapes and sizes. This is part of God's gift to his church. The fullness of his word pierces and cuts and changes people by addressing all manner of people in all the different circumstances of life. By the power of God's Spirit, we will preach the gospel clearly, truthfully and faithfully if we preach it by expounding God's word.

From the passage to the arrow

But now we need to think through the details of how to move from the passage to constructing the arrow. Perhaps the best way to start is by taking you through a week of my own sermon preparation. Let me tell you about the week I spent preparing to preach Matthew 5:13-16.[5]

I usually try to start preparing on Monday morning for the sermon that I will preach on the following Sunday. And I always start off by translating the passage. If you don't have the skills to do a translation, then make sure you read through the passage a number of times. One of the key things that translating helps me to do is slow down and read the passage carefully, so that I am responding to what's there rather than what is in my head. Here's the passage:

> "You are the salt of the earth, but if salt has lost its taste, how shall its saltiness be restored? It is no longer good for anything except to be thrown out and trampled under people's feet.
> "You are the light of the world. A city set on a hill cannot be hidden. Nor do people light a lamp and put it under a basket, but on a stand, and it gives light to all in the house. In the same way, let your light shine before others, so that they may see your good works and give glory to your Father who is in heaven." (Matt 5:13-16)

To tell you the truth, this is one of those truly wonderful Monday mornings. After translating the passage, I think to

---

5. In case there's any confusion, the 'I' in the following section is Phillip.

myself, "Marvellous! I've got a lot to do this week, and this is one of the easiest passages in the Bible. I know exactly how I'll preach this one. You're the salt—salt adds flavour and acts as a preservative. You're the light—light is knowledge. What you are is the salt, the preservative of society, the thing that adds flavour to society; and you're the light of the world—you are those who take the gospel out into the world. Here's a passage with world mission and social action all rolled into one." Every week is a hard week, and I give thanks for an easy passage.

But you know it isn't going to be that easy, don't you? Even as I congratulate myself on having the passage sorted so quickly, I remember reading somewhere that salt has something to do with purity and not just preservation. I guess if I'm going to be serious about preaching this passage, I really should look up a dictionary and see what salt was used for in the ancient world. So I take down a reference work on the ancient world and read the article on 'salt', only to find that there were many different uses for salt. They used salt to rub into babies; they used it to curse the land; they mixed it into manure; the priests used it in sacrifices; they used it in making covenants; they paid taxes with it. This raises the question in my mind. Why do I think of salt as being mainly about taste and preservation?

The question gets raised. But how do I answer it? The starting point is remembering that I'm just reading a dictionary about life in the ancient world. Sure, Jesus lived in that ancient world, but he lived as part of a particular culture—a culture built on the foundations of God's Old Testament word. So my next step is to think about what the Bible itself has to say about salt. My first port of call is a Bible dictionary, which is unfortunately very thin on salt, and so I decide to do what I should have done in the first place—which is to look up all the uses of salt in the Bible. How else will I know what God's word has to say about something without reading it? It's time to get the concordance out (or turn to my Bible software).

So I start ploughing my way through the Old Testament and it takes time (there are quite a lot of references to salt in there). And as I go, my frustration grows. Most of the many uses from the dictionary article are there plus a few more that I had never thought of—like Elisha using salt to turn the spring of bitter water into pure water (2 Kgs 2:19-22).

I know that Jesus was an Old Testament man, but which of the many possible Old Testament uses of salt was Jesus referring to when he talked about salt in Matthew 5? Of course, by this stage, it's no longer Monday morning. It's Wednesday morning and the church secretary is expecting the sermon outline by tomorrow lunchtime. But I can't preach what I don't understand, and so I keep wrestling with the text.

What's the next step? Rather than looking at the rest of the Bible, maybe I should just look at how Jesus uses the word 'salt'. So I work through the uses of salt in the teaching of Jesus, and the only other reference that seems in any way similar to Matthew 5 is in Luke 14:34-35. There Jesus talks about salt losing its saltiness. If the salt loses its saltiness, it is of no use for the manure pile. Now why would you put salt into a manure pile? It's certainly not about preservation or flavour! You put salt into manure in order to make fertilizer (and they still do it today). But what does that mean for Matthew 5? You are the manure pile stimulant of the world? And how does that relate to the light metaphor?

Having spent the first half of the week exploring what salt could or couldn't mean, I come to my first conclusion. You can't know on the basis of the other biblical references what Jesus was talking about. Now that's a big step forward, although it may not instantly look like it—or feel like it for that matter. But it's fundamental. When good research comes up with a negative answer, it helps you. It keeps you from being overconfident.

It holds you back from leaping to quick and convenient conclusions (like the one that I reached on Monday morning). It helps remove some of the assumptions and prejudices hidden in your initial (false) hypothesis. And it makes you look again at the passage you are studying.

If I can't know from the rest of the Bible what Jesus is saying, what course of action is left? Go back to the passage and read it again!

As I read, I notice that there aren't two images in the passage—salt and light. There are actually three images in the passage—salt, light and a city on a hill. Maybe the way forward is to examine the relationship between the three images. What are the three images about? That's not such a difficult question. They're about being unmistakable. They're about things that can't be hidden; things that have no point if they are hidden. Salt is no different to light or to the city on a hill. It is the immediate context and not the background or the imagery that brings us the meaning of the passage.

Jesus is saying to his disciples that they need to be radically and dramatically different. To be a true disciple of Jesus means being someone that can't be hidden. But that leads naturally to the next question: how are they to be radically and dramatically different? Anyone can be different, but how does Jesus want his disciples to be different? Again, I'm forced back to the passage and to the surrounding context.

Now, as I read the sections around the passage that I'm preaching, I notice the beatitudes, and in particular the change from the third person in Matthew 5:3-10—"blessed are those ... blessed are those ... blessed are those ..."—to the second person in verse 11—"blessed are you". Blessed are *you* when *you* are persecuted. And it suddenly begins to make sense—the beatitudes have all been leading up to the persecution of true disciples.

Why will the disciples be persecuted? Because they are so different from everyone else that they can't be hidden. What in particular will be different about them? Verse 16 has the answer: their good works will reveal them as those who belong to God and live for his glory. These good works are what the rest of chapter 5 is all about—dealing with their anger; resisting their lust; keeping their word; loving their enemies.

Finally I'm starting to get somewhere. Jesus is talking to his disciples about what it means to be his disciples. Suddenly the salt of the earth fits into the context of the rest of the narrative. But all of this thinking leads me closer and closer to understanding the Sermon on the Mount. Where and when does Jesus speak these words? "Seeing the crowds, he went up on the mountain, and when he sat down, his disciples came to him" (Matt 5:1). The whole sermon is preached to his disciples in the midst of the crowds.

So we need to ask: who are the crowds? And the answer is found in the final verses of chapter 4:

> And he went throughout all Galilee, teaching in their synagogues and proclaiming the gospel of the kingdom and healing every disease and every affliction among the people. So his fame spread throughout all Syria, and they brought him all the sick, those afflicted with various diseases and pains, those oppressed by demons, epileptics, and paralytics, and he healed them. And great crowds followed him from Galilee and the Decapolis, and from Jerusalem and Judea, and from beyond the Jordan. (Matt 4:23-25)

That's the kind of verse I'd usually skip straight past. It's Friday lunchtime and I still haven't got the outline to the secretary, but I have no choice now but to keep going. I get the map out and look at the locations that are mentioned. Matthew doesn't give us numbers but he does tell us how diverse the crowd is, and how far away people are coming from. Jesus' ministry has become so famous that people are travelling literally weeks in order to come and see him.

Finally, the pieces are coming together. Jesus is healing people and the crowds are travelling from all over the known world to come and see him. So what does he do? He takes his disciples up on the hill and he starts to teach them. And what does he teach them? Blessed are you when everyone hates you. Blessed are you when your life looks so different from the world that it cannot be hidden. Blessed are you when your good works mark you out as a disciple.

The disciples need to know what real discipleship is in the midst of the fame and excitement of the crowds because, as Jesus will remind them in Matthew 7, there is a big difference between being one of the crowd and entering the kingdom of heaven:

> "Enter by the narrow gate. For the gate is wide and the way is easy that leads to destruction, and those who enter by it are many. For the gate is narrow and the way is hard that leads to life, and those who find it are few ...
>
> "Not everyone who says to me, 'Lord, Lord,' will enter the kingdom of heaven, but the one who does the will of my Father who is in heaven. On that day many will say to me, 'Lord, Lord, did we not prophesy in your name, and cast out demons in your name, and do many mighty works in your name?' And then I will declare to them, 'I never knew you; depart from me, you workers of lawlessness'." (Matt 7:13-14, 21-23)

Having called the disciples out to be fishers of men, Jesus begins his ministry, and it is hugely successful—there are people coming from everywhere. But Jesus chooses that very moment to take his disciples aside to tell them that the great crowds are not the heart of his ministry. What is really important to Jesus is being so changed by the truth that you do the kind of good works that people will hate you for.

Now, how do you turn all of that into a sermon? Before I answer that, let's tease out a number of general principles for sermon preparation, in light of the process that I've just described to you.

Principles for preparation
1. Start with the text and end with the text
The most vital lesson to be learned is the importance of letting the text say what the text has to say. While the original sermon that I wanted to preach about social action and evangelism wouldn't have been a bad thing to say, it wouldn't have been what God was actually saying in this passage. And it is only by letting the passage ask hard questions of us that we are saved from preaching our hobbyhorses and our comfortably well-worn systematic theology. This is not to denigrate systematic theology, which is in fact vitally important (we'll come back to this in the next chapter). But it is to point out that our system always feels comfortable to us because it is our system. And our sinfulness will always mean that our system is deficient. We stand in constant need of correction. As you preach the sermon that you would never have thought to preach after reading the passage for the first time, your system will be truly shaped by God's word.

Therefore, at the very nitty-gritty functional level, work hard at reading the passage slowly and carefully. Note where the passage says things that you weren't expecting it to say; observe the change from the third person to the second person in the beatitudes; notice the fact that there are three images—salt, light and the city on a hill; pay attention to the broader context, and keep asking whether your understanding of the passage makes sense in the broader flow of the narrative or argument.

Given the busyness of pastoral ministry and the pressure to be seen to be doing all the things that your congregation thinks you should be doing, it is very easy to short-change the sermon preparation process. One of the easiest shortcuts of all involves preaching what we hope that the passage is saying rather than what it is actually saying. When you come across something that is unexpected, make the time to work it out. In particular contexts, this may even mean patiently teaching your congregation that you're as much use to them as you sit in your study unravelling the riches of God's word as you are out visiting the sick.

2. Use your external sources wisely

The second thing to point out is the place of external aids in the process of preparation. It is very easy, particularly after spending years in seminary or Bible college, to assume that the answers we need will be found in the finest writers of the day. And so in order to find out what the text says we spend more time in the biggest, fattest, most up-to-date commentaries than we do in the Bible itself. But even the writers of the very best commentaries don't know more about God's will than the apostles who penned God's word. And God's revelation is not in their commentary but in the original text.

Part of the problem arises from the process by which commentaries come to be written these days. It starts with university staff and postgraduate scholars producing monographs, theses and journal articles, usually about a small point in the text or an obscure matter of current debate. The pressure on these scholars (in respect of their jobs and careers) is to say something new, and this tends to push them towards historical background research—an area in which it is easier to come up with new discoveries and to contribute to the ongoing academic conversation. The commentary writers then gather up these various articles and theses into a book that is really a compendium of recent research organized by the text of a Bible book. The commentators will usually try to add something to the research by giving an overall argument to the book, but frequently they do no more than arbitrate among the various articles and debates, very often losing sight of the message and emphasis of the biblical text as they do so.

The result is that the agenda for the conversation has been set by someone apart from God. And in modern theological writing, it has often been set by someone who has no idea at all about who God is, but who has been asked to write the commentary because of their status or experience within the academic community.

It's not that we should ignore the commentaries. They can be very useful tools, especially in pointing out interesting things in the text that we wouldn't have noticed otherwise. And if they have theological biases and commitments different from our own, they can lead us to ask questions that we would never have asked. But never read commentaries until you have wrestled with the text for yourself, and come to some conclusions about what you think and why. Otherwise you will just lap up whatever they feed you.

Commentaries, Bible dictionaries and the like are great servants but lousy masters.

3. Always wrestle with the biblical context

Every time we preach a passage, we preach it within the context of larger wholes. A few verses in a certain book are part of a chapter. Most often, that chapter is part of a larger group of chapters that make up a book. The book sits either in the New or the Old Testament and, finally, within the unfolding sweep of the 66 infallible books of God's revealed word. Therefore good preaching will always involve reading the passage in light of the larger whole.

When a passage quotes another part of the Scriptures, always go there and look at the quote in its original context. Once you have decided what a particular passage means, ask whether it makes sense in the light of the rest of the book. Always keep working at understanding the context not just of what you are reading, but of the whole book, testament and Bible.

In the case we have looked at above, the concordance study of 'salt' in the Old Testament might have seemed like a waste of time, but it wasn't. It was part of remembering that the Bible is the context of every other part of God's word. Even the process of looking up the verses throughout the Bible forces us to read other parts of God's word. That labour will never be in vain. Furthermore, the electronic Bible study tools that are now available make the process much more accessible than it has ever been before. We really have no excuse for avoiding the hard work of wrestling with biblical meaning for ourselves.

It was only as I came back to Matthew 5:13-16 and wrestled with it again and again in its own context that I began to see the main points that God was making in his word.

4. There is no substitute for hard work

All of this means that there are no shortcuts or easy ways to produce faithful, clear sermons. Good sermon preparation always involves hard, prayerful work on the text—the work of translating and thinking and reflecting and turning up other passages and asking the hard questions and wrestling to understand what God wants to say. If you're afraid of hard work, then you shouldn't be preaching regularly.

5. The hard work is cumulative

The good news is that the hard work is cumulative. Each time you do a word study, and each time you work passage by passage through a book of the Bible, God is shaping your heart and your mind. The next time you come back to preach this book, you will already have done much of the background thinking. You will be able to stop and pay attention to the parts you didn't quite understand last time around. When I preach now, it is not just the fruit of the last week spent in the study, but the last forty years of preaching the Bible. Good preachers, who spend their lives grappling with God's word, become better and better preachers over time.

6. Let the logic of the text shape the sermon

But before we finish the chapter, let's return to the question of moving from the text to the sermon, because letting the text shape the sermon isn't just about understanding the main points that the text has to make. It's also about understanding the logic and structure of the biblical argument and working out how that should shape what you actually say when you get up to preach.

Logic and structure are not always exactly the same thing. For example in the first part of the Sermon on the Mount (Matt 5:1-16) there is quite a clear structure. There is an introductory verse that sets the scene (v. 1). Then there are the beatitudes (vv. 2-12). Then Jesus talks about salt, light and the city on the hill (vv. 13-16). This structure is so clear that you might even create your sermon series based around the structure—preaching Matthew 5:1-12 in the first week, Matthew 5:13-16 the next week, and so on.

But as we've seen above, the logic of the passage doesn't quite match the structure. For example, verses 11-12 are about the blessings of being persecuted for Christ. Structurally they occur as one of the beatitudes, but they are logically connected to the following verses, which explain why you would be persecuted for Jesus—because you have done distinctively different, God-glorifying, good works. The key then is not just to preach the structure or to highlight the structure but to make sense of the logic, and to let the logic work its way out in the sermon.

So what is the logic of this part of the Sermon on the Mount?

1. Jesus' ministry has drawn a crowd to see his healings, and so Jesus retires to the mountain to teach his disciples.
2. He teaches his disciples that being a part of the kingdom of God is not what they expect: it is about being meek, poor, pure in heart, and so on.
3. Most importantly it is about being someone who is so committed to Jesus that you will be persecuted.
4. And you will be persecuted because you are so different from those around you in the good works that you perform.
5. This gives glory to your Father in heaven.

One possible structure for a sermon on this passage would follow this logical outline, but it doesn't have to. There is another issue involved. How do you structure a sermon so as to *communicate* this logic to those who are listening? And how do you engage your listeners in order to see the significance of what God is saying to them?

I decided that the best way to preach this passage would be to take my congregation into my week. So I started out by talking about the salt and light parables and how I, just like they, have heard them lots of times and think that I have a fair grasp on what they mean. But I was wrong. I started the week thinking the passage meant something and ended it realizing that the passage said something else. By taking my congregation into my week, I was teaching them that even their pastor was learning new things from the Bible. That sent a message to the congregation that I was still learning, just like they are.

Then I took the time to show them the entries in the dictionary and the Old Testament that referred to salt. This was to teach them to keep reading the Bible, and to show them that what the Bible says is more important than the external sources. Finally I brought them back to the passage and showed them the three images in verses 13-16 (salt, light and city on a hill), and pointed out that it's about being distinctively different.

All of this created a platform for me to show them the broader logic of the passage—Jesus, in the midst of his fame, took his disciples aside to tell them that real kingdom living is about godliness that results in persecution. The crux of the sermon then becomes the question: are you a useless disciple? If Jesus says that real disciples are so different that they suffer, then the right question to ask is: are you different enough that you suffer?[6]

In the process of putting any sermon together, one of the big questions in my mind is: how much of my hard work in exegesis and understanding do I have to show the congregation in the sermon for them to understand the logic of the passage and feel the weight of the conclusion?

It largely depends on the congregation you're preaching to. In some cases, I would not use the dictionary references or the Old Testament references in the sermon to make the point that you can't work out what salt means. It might be just as effective (and shorter) to show people that there are three images here that all have something in common. But then you lose the lessons about external sources and how to read the Bible.

Whatever you decide to do in the end, the key is to work out how to structure your sermon in a way that *so conveys the logic of the text that the congregation feels the weight of the conclusion.*

---

6. To listen to the sermon in question, go to www.matthiasmedia.com.au/rd.html?sku=aata and download the talk on Matthew 5:13-16.

Sometimes that will involve sticking very closely to the structure of the biblical text. At other times, it will mean finding a different structure for your sermon that respects the structure of the text and yet makes the logic clear for the hearer. For example, my sermon on Matthew started with the point about salt and worked backwards through the passage, but hopefully in such a way that people heard loudly and clearly at the end what it means to be a disciple of Jesus who lives for the kingdom of God.

The arrow the passage produced

As we draw the chapter to a close, let's remember our arrow diagram. The head of the arrow built around Matthew 5 was the call to live differently as servants of the kingdom—to do God-glorifying good works that cannot be hidden. In order to deliver that head to its target, I crafted a shaft that showed people the main exegetical points in the passage (i.e. the set of three distinctive things in verses 13-16 and the blessings that come to those who are persecuted). And the feathers, in this case, were the wider context of Matthew's Gospel: on the one hand this meant pointing out that Jesus taught his disciples about true discipleship as they were confronted by the fame of his ministry, and on the other hand it meant pointing out that the nature of distinctive good works was spelled out in the rest of chapter 5, which we would be looking at in the weeks to come.

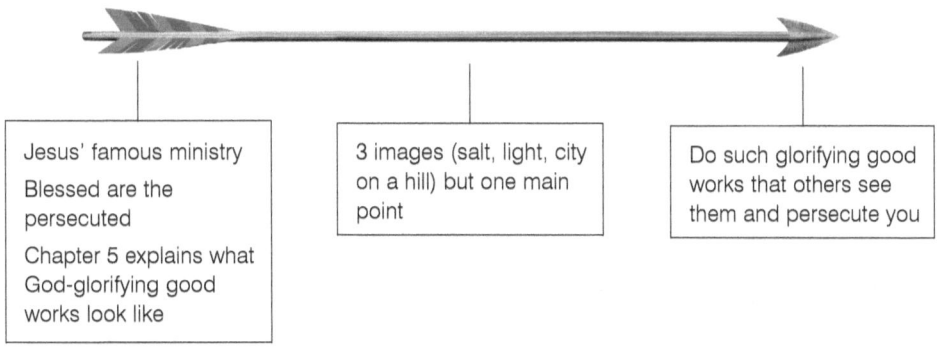

This is all much easier to say than it is to do. But with practice it is possible to get better at doing it. And as we get better at preaching the logic of the text and helping people to feel the weight of its conclusions, we are actually working at saying what God wants to say to his people—the primary goal of the preacher.

Chapter 4

On the importance of feathers

Most preachers who choose to call themselves 'evangelical' would also like to claim the label 'simple Bible preacher'. It is a profoundly attractive label. It speaks of a transparency and a commitment to the biblical text that is sadly lacking in many pulpits today. It tells your listeners that you haven't been whitewashed by the lifeless ramblings of liberalism—you haven't let academic pretensions or the thoughts of sinful man invade your desire to speak God's words.

However, applying the label is often also an exercise in naivety. It is too easily applied while assuming that we are uniquely unaffected by our culture, history, family or sinfulness. We need to realize that it is impossible to come to the text of the Bible independent of our own presuppositions, whether good or bad. The problem with claiming to be a 'simple Bible preacher' is that it results in a lack of personal reflection—a lack of reflection that often leads to a misreading of the Bible. It leads us to find what we want to find and what we expect to find, rather than what is actually written there.

I may think I know what this passage is about before I even come to preach it—and my father and my father's father may have read it the same way—but this is no guarantee that I'm correct. While some theological traditions do reflect a more biblical world view than others, we are fooling ourselves (and our hearers) if we think that our tradition brings us untarnished to the word of God. All of this is to say that in our model of the arrow the feathers are vitally important. Every arrow will be affected by the quality of its feathers. It will either fly straight and true, or deviate in one direction or another, because of the feathers that have been attached.

Because every sermon has feathers attached, whether knowingly or not, one mark that distinguishes the good preacher from other preachers is the ability to understand how the preacher's own feathers have affected the shaping of his arrows. If we're honest, most of our arrows are fitted with the feathers that we like best—the ones plucked from our own tail. Our favourite topics, our frustrations with those we minister to, our understanding of the world's great problems and needs, and our personal experiences of pain—we bring all of these (and more) to our preaching. They affect the books or passages that we choose to speak from, and the sermons we craft from those chosen sections of Scripture. This is fundamentally true of all preachers.

But because we are human beings, our tail-feathers are as tainted by sin as the rest of us. And so our arrows will be plagued by the tendency to deviate in the direction least likely to pierce our own misunderstandings and sins. The only possible solution to this problem is to acknowledge the existence of our tail-feathers, and to expose them to corrective pruning or even plucking by God's word—a painful but necessary process.

As faithful preachers we must put aside the illusion that we are unpolluted sponges, ready to soak up God's word and squeeze it out, pure and fresh, for our adoring listeners. We must work hard at shaping our own systematic and biblical theology in the light of what God actually says. Good preachers must be good biblical and systematic theologians.

Let's explore what this will mean.

Being a systematic theologian

For many, becoming a good systematic theologian means reading Augustine, Athanasius, Anselm, Calvin, Luther, Baxter, Edwards, Barth, Berkhof, Grudem, Moltmann and Wright (or whatever selection of famous theologians happens to be approved or encouraged within their chosen tradition), and then deftly selecting the appropriate passage from the appropriate author in order to make their sermons sound more learned. While a good systematic theologian will benefit greatly from reading the thoughts of others, their most profound task is not to assimilate another's thinking but to understand God and his world through God's own eyes.

That is why Calvin is possibly the greatest systematician (apart from the apostles) in the history of Christian thought. Calvin's *Institutes of the Christian Religion* began life in 1536 as a short tract designed to introduce theological students to the Bible, and reached its final form in 1559. The final version was almost five times the length of the original. In between the four extensive revisions and expansions over the course of its life, Calvin wrote commentaries on nearly all the books of the Bible and preached day by day through the Scriptures. His systematic theology—his understanding of God and his world—was thoroughly informed by a close reading of the individual texts of the Bible. While Calvin read and interacted with many of the Church Fathers, his systematic theology was founded on his interactions with God's word.

But it is instructive to understand how Calvin thought about the process of reading the Bible and thinking theologically. The *Institutes* were written to be an introduction to reading the Bible:

> I may add, that my object in this work was to prepare and
> train students of theology for the study of the sacred
> volume, so that they might both have an easy introduction

to it, and be able to proceed in it, with unfaltering step, seeing I have endeavoured to give such a summary of religion in all its parts, and have digested it into such an order as may make it not difficult for any one, who is rightly acquainted with it, to ascertain both what he ought principally to look for in Scripture, and also to what head he ought to refer whatever is contained in it.[7]

Calvin was convinced that in order to read the Bible properly, people must understand the key ideas and main themes of Scripture. He believed that if you introduced theological students to the key themes of Scripture, then they would read the Bible well.

It's an approach guaranteed to fill us with fear and trepidation. Surely starting with Calvin's ideas will warp and shape the way we read the Bible! Isn't he in danger of teaching his own system rather than the word of God?

Of course he is. But the objection misses the point. Presuppositions are involved in the reading of any book—not only our own presuppositions and world view, but also those of the author. The key to reading any author well is to be aware of our own presuppositions *and* the author's, and then to keep reading in light of those.

Calvin realized that we need to read the Bible sympathetically, something that we can only do by assuming the framework of thought of the author—in this case, God. In other words, we read the Bible and preach it well when we possess certain fundamental convictions about it—for example, when we believe that the Bible is the word of God that brings life and salvation to all. And we know that the Bible is read badly when

---

7. J Calvin, 'Epistle to the Reader (Calvin, 1539)', in *Institutes of the Christian Religion*, tr. H Beveridge, rev. edn, Hendrickson, Peabody, 2008, p. xxxiv. Available online (viewed 17 June 2009): www.ccel.org/ccel/calvin/institutes.ii.ix.html

certain convictions *aren't* held. For example, the atheist who comes to the Scriptures in order to be sceptical, disobedient and hard-hearted will consistently misread God's word.

It is vitally important that we understand this point in particular. In our rationalist, scientific world, we are constantly encouraged to believe in the myth of neutrality—most often expressed as the importance of the observer remaining objective. How many times have we been told that the historian or the scientist approaches the Bible more truly than the theologian? But we cannot approach the Bible with complete neutrality, and we shouldn't want to. God tells us to read the Bible not neutrally but obediently.

The good news is that God's word is more powerful than our disobedience. The sword of God's Spirit is able to break through even the most hard-hearted scepticism and bring people to faith and life. Your framework for reading can be changed by what you read in the Bible! But it is also true that at the point of regeneration, people begin to read the Bible differently. And this leads us to the second main point.

Our biblical framework—our doctrine—needs to keep growing and being shaped as we read God's word. Calvin's *Institutes* were expanded and developed in the context of hard exegetical work on the text of Scripture. What was true for Calvin is true for all of us. As people grow in Christian maturity, and read and understand more of the Bible for themselves, they become better readers of the Bible. This is because the Bible does actually mean something. We may need to avoid the myth of neutral objectivity, but we also don't wish to fall into the opposite and very common error these days of postmodern relativism—that the text has no objective meaning, but is like a mirror that simply reflects back the beliefs and presuppositions of the reader. The obedient reader does not supply meaning to the text, but reads and listens to the meaning that God the author is conveying in the text.

What all this means in practice is that good preaching will occur when we read the Bible doctrinally and when we evaluate our doctrine biblically.

Let's look at a practical example of what this might mean by turning to the next section of the Sermon on the Mount.

> "Do not think that I have come to abolish the Law or the Prophets; I have not come to abolish them but to fulfill them. For truly, I say to you, until heaven and earth pass away, not an iota, not a dot, will pass from the Law until all is accomplished. Therefore whoever relaxes one of the least of these commandments and teaches others to do the same will be called least in the kingdom of heaven, but whoever does them and teaches them will be called great in the kingdom of heaven. For I tell you, unless your righteousness exceeds that of the scribes and Pharisees, you will never enter the kingdom of heaven."
> (Matt 5:17-20)

There are a number of significant issues raised by this passage. But the one most keenly felt by many preachers is the problem presented by verse 20: "For I tell you, unless your righteousness exceeds that of the scribes and Pharisees, you will never enter the kingdom of heaven". Given that the Pharisees were the law-keepers *par excellence*, what does this passage mean for the Christian? Can we really say that unless we are better law-keepers than the Pharisees we will never enter the kingdom of heaven?

Neither of the two obvious solutions to the problem is particularly satisfactory. On the one hand, we could push the 'face value' of Jesus' words to their extreme and call on people to double their human efforts to gain salvation. On the other hand, we could retreat into our systematic theology too quickly by pointing out that the righteousness Jesus demands leads to an impossibly high standard that can only be met by faith in his death.

The problem with the first solution is the violence it does to so much of the rest of the New Testament. Our works cannot make us right with God (e.g. Rom 3:20; Gal 2:16). The problem with the second solution is that it ends up neutering Jesus' commands. He is intent on doing more than just pointing out our sinfulness in this section. Jesus doesn't just say that being angry is the same as committing murder; he also says, therefore go and be reconciled with your brother. He doesn't just tell us that retaliation is evil, but that we should go out of our way to do good to our enemies.

Far from saying that works don't matter, Jesus declares that doing and teaching the law is fundamental to kingdom greatness: "whoever relaxes one of the least of these commandments and teaches others to do the same will be called least in the kingdom of heaven, but whoever does them and teaches them will be called great in the kingdom of heaven" (Matt 5:19). While we do not want to preach the passage in such a way that it encourages us to works righteousness—as if human beings could ever lay claim on God—neither do we wish to say any less than Jesus actually says.

At this point, whether we like it or not, we are deeply engaged in a theological exercise. As faithful preachers we must think about how Jesus' words interact with the rest of God's revelation and with the lives of those we are preaching to. There is no 'non-theological' solution.

We will come to one possible solution shortly, but simply acknowledging that there is an issue to grapple with is the vital first step. The very fact that we have stopped and acknowledged that there is a problem not easily solved by either of our original knee-jerk reactions, has put us in a place where we will wrestle again with God's word. That is never a vain activity, because God promises to give us his Spirit so that we will truly know him.

This is not, by the way, some glib promise—as if following the 'correct' method will always guarantee the right answer. The promise of the Spirit is not a promise of preacherly infallibility. But it is a promise of great comfort. God looks graciously upon those who stand before him humble and contrite in spirit (Isa 66:2). As we kneel before his word and long to understand his wisdom, he will grant us insight. It will be a stop-start process, governed at every point by the grace of God. But years of doing the hard work of attempting to understand, obey and apply God's word will result in clearer preaching.

However, back to the problem with preaching Matthew 5. What are we to make of Jesus' words about being possessed by Pharisee-surpassing righteousness? The answer lies in assuming that Jesus meant to say what he said, and then working out how to integrate that with the big picture of God's work in salvation.

Jesus never intended to encourage his hearers to trust in their righteousness, but he also meant to challenge people to real obedience. The punch line of the entire Sermon on the Mount is found at its end where Jesus challenges his hearers to build on the rock and not the sand. "Everyone then who hears these words of mine *and does them* will be like a wise man who built his house on the rock" (Matt 7:24). Jesus wants his hearers to know that those in the kingdom acknowledge him as king in the way they live.

The big question then, is how does that happen? How does someone come to call Jesus their Lord? In the famous Old Testament chapters, Ezekiel 36 and Jeremiah 31, God made absolutely clear that the great problem with the old covenant was not his word but the disobedient, hard-heartedness of his people (cf. Hebrews 8). God promised in both of these passages that a day was coming when he would change the hearts of his people, and in Ezekiel he explicitly said that the change would occur by the work of his life-giving Spirit.

When we come to the New Testament, Jesus Christ dies and rises again as the Lord and Saviour of the world and pours out his Spirit in order to bring people to him. Only through the work of the Spirit can people turn from living for themselves to living with Jesus as their king. And only by spiritual new-birth can people be transformed to live for the glory of God.

One of the central marks of this change will be exactly what Jesus describes in Matthew 5—not a desire to tame the word of God so as to justify ourselves in spite of our disobedience, but a Spirit-fuelled change that leads us to long to serve God and do his will in every part of life. A person who has been changed by the Spirit of God, to live with Jesus as their Lord, will be transformed to delight in maximal obedience to him—they will fulfil the law in love. As Paul summarizes it later in the New Testament:

> Owe no-one anything, except to love each other, for the one who loves another has fulfilled the law. For the commandments, "You shall not commit adultery, You shall not murder, You shall not steal, You shall not covet," and any other commandment, are summed up in this word: "You shall love your neighbor as yourself". Love does no wrong to a neighbor; therefore love is the fulfilling of the law. (Rom 13:8-10)

A robust theology of the lordship of Jesus and the work of the Holy Spirit, and a clear understanding of God's goal—to glorify himself by creating a people who will glorify him by their good works—are necessary if we are to preach Matthew 5 faithfully.

With those theological building blocks in place, we are free to say what Jesus says within the context of God's gospel. A healthy systematic theology will mean that we are able to point out that the Sermon on the Mount sets an unattainable standard that drives us to Jesus—without blunting Jesus' main point that those who know him will live with a transformed understanding of righteousness.

The pharisaic approach to righteousness was to domesticate and minimize the requirements of the law so that they could be seen to obey it. This is what Jesus is preaching against. If we want to preach what Jesus was teaching in this part of the Sermon on the Mount, people must hear that kingdom-dwellers won't limit their concept of righteousness so that the Pharisee within them is able to obey it.

Furthermore, God's people ought to walk away from this passage longing to hear and obey Jesus' words. But we will only be able to say these things in a way that doesn't distort the gospel if we have a clear, theological grasp of the gospel.

You may still have ongoing questions about how to communicate these truths in the context of a sermon.[8] But that is not our particular concern in this chapter. Our original point was that a preacher needs to be a self-conscious systematic theologian. Hopefully Matthew 5 has made what that means a little clearer.

Before we move on, it is worth reflecting on some practical ways to develop ourselves theologically.

1. Keep reading the Bible

The source of all our theology must be the word of God, and so the most obvious but often overlooked way to develop our theology is to read broadly and thoughtfully in the Bible. If you want to improve your systematic theology, ensure that you are regularly reading through the Bible and being constantly exposed to God's thinking about subjects that you would otherwise avoid. If there are parts of the Bible you feel uncomfortable about, then make an extra effort to read and preach those sections.

---

8. For an example of how it can be done, go to www.matthiasmedia.com.au/rd.html?sku=aata and download the talk on Matthew 5:17-30.

2. Rejoice when you don't understand the Bible

Sermon preparation is a great balancing act amidst the busyness of ministry life. Many practical dilemmas arise every week. Should you spend time locating interesting illustrations, or thinking about concrete applications, or wrestling with the theological difficulties that the passage presents?

Most pastors, by the time they're preaching regularly, have already given some thought to the big theological questions and formed some sort of answer to them (see further below on the importance of theological education). They know where they stand on predestination, the nature of justification, the place of men and women in ministry, the role of the Holy Spirit, and many other biblical truths. So, given the importance of evangelism, personal ministry and the administration required to keep the wheels turning, stopping to think again about these topics feels time-consuming and relatively unimportant. If the passage says something that doesn't fit into our theological picture, it is quicker and easier to explain it away than to stop and think about why God's word says what it says.

But somehow we need to build into our sermon preparation the time to stop and explore new ideas. When the Bible doesn't say what we want it to say, we need to be able to ask questions and do some more reading and thinking and praying. If we always gloss over the parts of the Bible we find difficult or uncomfortable, we will end up as perpetual Christian infants, leading a congregation of babes in Christ.

When the passage disagrees with our theology it ought to be a source of rejoicing. Here is an opportunity to repent and grow in our knowledge of God's truth.

3. Pursue formal theological education

Having spent much time and space speaking about the importance of letting the Bible shape our theological convictions, it is nevertheless important to acknowledge the flip side of this coin. Calvin was right to give his students a biblical framework for reading the Bible, because it is ultimately impossible to read the Bible without presuppositions.

This is why the primary theological education we receive in our families and in our churches is so important. And it is also why formal theological education is so vital for those who are to become full-time pastors and preachers. A formal theological education is not a small investment. It typically requires three to four years of your life, usually at a time when family responsibilities have increased and when your opportunities for ministry are growing. Given the urgency of the task, why bother spending all of this time in theological education?

The answer lies in the importance and complexity of the theological task. Holding together the great truths of God's word in such a way that they are clearly articulated and faithfully applied is no small task—and yet it is a vital one. Many pastors who have started out with zeal have ended up shipwrecking their faith by letting their theological position be pushed around by the rough and tumble of pastoral life and personal evangelism. Holding onto the truth in the midst of the pragmatic challenges of keeping even a small church running is a difficult exercise.

Theological education provides a foundation and framework for further thinking as well as providing the tools to keep growing in your doctrine. An understanding of the original languages and exposure to a variety of theological positions, in a context where these are biblically critiqued and explored, gives a person the foundations they need to keep working on their theology for the rest of their life.

A good theological education should teach people how to think. Depending on your background and prior education, it may need to teach you how to read and interact with texts in their original languages, and provide you with some background in philosophy and western intellectual history. History, philosophy, historical theology, ethics, language study—these supporting subjects in a theological education are often somewhat despised by the keen young theological student who is eager to be studying the Bible, and even more eager to be done with theological education and out into ministry. But these sorts of subjects are enormously useful for the preacher as he seeks to understand and preach God's word in a particular cultural context, and explain to his hearers how the thinking and world view of the Bible differs from and critiques the thought-forms and world views of our age. They are very useful, in other words, for adding feathers to his arrow so that it flies straight and true to the hearts of his hearers.

A sound theological education will introduce us to topics and ideas that we might not have chosen to think about, nor even have been aware of. It should show us how to listen carefully and thoughtfully to what another person has to say by seeking to understand their thinking and world view. And it will also encourage students to critique their own opinions and others in light of Scripture. Most of all, and most importantly of all, it should increase our knowledge of the God whom we serve through Jesus Christ.

4. Pursue theological education for the rest of your life

A good theological education will equip pastors to keep growing and learning so that they are able to teach God's word in real-life situations, which they had never even imagined encountering while in seminary. But that is why theological education is not just about the years spent in formal study. Nobody can learn in three or four years all that is required for a lifetime of ministry. Every pastor understands the difference between life in an academic institution and life in the real world. Being able to discuss the various differences of opinion amongst theologians through the ages is not quite the same thing as deciding what biblical advice you will give to those who come to you with serious pastoral issues.

Understanding what other writers and thinkers have said and why they have said it provides the framework for coming to your own decisions about difficult moral and ethical issues. However, it is often only in the practice of pastoral ministry that the answers to these questions become more than academic. The skills learned in college need to be developed as you pastor the congregation God has given you to love. A good preacher will aim to be continually developing theologically so as also to develop pastorally.

One of the keys to doing this is disciplining yourself to read widely. Some wisdom is required here. Young preachers will be better served by reading classic Reformation and evangelical works of theology. This is a time to put in place foundation stones, and to get a grasp of the foundations of biblical truth. But as time goes on, we need to work at reading people who are not from our theological stable—authors who ask questions that we would never think to ask, and who press us to articulate, from the Bible, why we believe what we believe.

The preacher who is committed to continually learning, repenting and growing in their doctrine will be the pastor whose leadership and teaching is still faithful in 30 years time. Real preaching—preaching that engages with the word of God and the lives of the hearers—is always theological preaching. Good exegetical preaching will always be theologically aware preaching.

Let's move on to look at the importance of biblical theology for preaching.

Being a biblical theologian

There has been a long and complicated debate going back decades, if not centuries, about what 'biblical theology' is exactly.

It's not going to help us to delve into the intricacies of that discussion here. It is more important to understand how some form of biblical theology will help us be better preachers.

The way we are using the term, 'biblical theology' means basically two things. First, it is the acknowledgement that the Bible unfolds as a progressive revelation. When God spoke to Abraham, the fullness of his character and the details of his plans for creation were not known in the way that they were subsequently revealed through the apostles. For this reason, biblical Bible reading always involves remembering where we are up to in God's unfolding plan for his world. The way that we make sense of Deuteronomy and apply it to God's people will be different from the way we read Philippians and seek to live it out today.

The second, and much more significant insight of biblical theology is that all of the promises of God find their yes and amen in Christ (2 Cor 1:20). We have already covered some of the important ground here as we looked at what it means for the preacher to "preach the gospel by prayerfully expounding the Bible" in chapters 2 and 3. If the central message of the Bible is the plan of God to reconcile the whole world under Christ, then we cannot ultimately preach any part of that word without reference to God's eternal plan fulfilled in him. Good preaching is gospel preaching from both the Old and New Testaments.

This insight into the place of Christ in understanding God's promises is crucial for preachers to grasp because of its implications for how to apply the Bible today—a particularly fraught issue in any theology of preaching.[9]

The great problem that both moderns and postmoderns have had with the text of the Bible is that they regard it as being

---

9. For more on this, see the article 'Herman who?', *The Briefing*, no. 4, June 1988. Available online: www.matthiasmedia.com.au/briefing/library/1270/

trapped in its own time and its own conventions. Many would argue that in order for the Bible to speak to us today, we must find ways of bridging the 2000-year gap between Christ and us (not to mention the 3000 plus years that separate us from Moses).

That gap has been crossed in many ways. Some have demythologized, some have moralized, some have found their own particular mystical meaning, some have read against the grain—finding the lost feminist or liberationist reading that really should have been there in the first place. But what has been assumed by all and sundry is that whatever it might mean today, it most probably won't be what it meant back when God first said it.

Biblical theology, by its very nature, addresses this misunderstanding head on. Biblical theology contends that the word of God is ultimately the word of *God* to us (1 Cor 10:11). Therefore, whatever we may notice about the various circumstances and personalities of the human authors, the Bible is ultimately the one word of the one heavenly author. It is the story of God's dealings with his creation, within which we find God making promises and fulfilling them. These promises and their fulfilment reveal the meaning of life in God's world.

If we take this understanding of the Bible seriously, then the divisions that we make between life in the 21st century and life in the first century aren't nearly as significant as they first seem. According to the Scriptures, there has been one great dividing line in history—the line between BC and AD. That is the one theologically significant division in human history.

Before the coming of Christ, God's plans for the world were only revealed in embryo. Daniel was told that God's words were shut up and sealed until the end of time (Dan 12:8-9). Peter reminds us that the prophets searched and inquired carefully into "what person or time the Spirit of Christ in them was indicating when he predicted the sufferings of Christ and subsequent glories". But "it was revealed to them that they were serving not themselves but you, in the things that have now been announced to you through those who preached the good news to you by the Holy Spirit sent from heaven" (1 Pet 1:11-12). God's plans for the world were spoken in promise, but have now been fulfilled in Christ. What was once hidden has now been revealed (Eph 3:1-13).

And so the coming of Christ marks a huge change in history. Instead of people coming to know God by becoming a part of Israel, all people—Jews and Gentiles alike—now come to know God by the gospel of Jesus Christ. The dividing wall of hostility is abolished. The old age gives way to the new, as God's promise to transform hearts and minds becomes a reality through the outpouring of the Spirit by the resurrected Christ. There is no greater disruption in the nature of the universe than the transition that occurs between the Old and New Testaments.

And yet in spite of such a great, God-given transformation between the ages, the people of the new covenant are to read the Old Testament as their book. The early believers did not need to bridge the many centuries between themselves and Moses; they just needed to understand the word of God revealed in the Old Testament in the light of the coming of Christ. What separated first-century Greeks from the Hebrews who lived 2000 years before them was not their language or their culture—it was Christ. And so new covenant believers, whether Jews or Gentiles, were expected to read the Old Testament as their own, because it is the shadow that makes sense of the fulfilment, who is Christ (Heb 10:1, 11:39-40). Furthermore, Christ so fulfils the Old Testament that anyone can read and understand it once they have come to know him.

What becomes clear is that the gospel is God's word to all. It is the word to Jew and Gentile, to male and female, to barbarian, Scythian, slave and free, because it makes known that God's plan has always been for the salvation of all people. The fundamental reality that binds us together as human beings is our common descent from Adam, our sinful disobedience that needs forgiveness, and our place in God's plan to glorify his Son.

There is certainly a significant advance in understanding of the old covenant in Christ, and this affects the application of the Old Testament word to the believer. But it has nothing to do with the kinds of innovations that are currently put forward as modern solutions for reading the ancient text.

As Psalm 95 is read out in 21st century New York, London, Beijing or Jerusalem, the Holy Spirit says: "Today, if you hear his voice, do not harden your hearts" (Heb 3:7-8). A Christian approach to hermeneutics has very little to do with what the academy does with ancient texts, but everything to do with how the Scriptures interpret themselves. The events of Israel's wilderness experience "happened to them as an example, but they were written down for our instruction, on whom the end of the ages has come" (1 Cor 10:11).

And so the apostles preached the one true word of God—the gospel of the death and resurrection of Christ—to everyone that they came across, because the fundamental realities for all human beings had changed. With the resurrection of Jesus, the day of judgement was set (Acts 17:30-31), and we entered into the urgency of the last days, in which the real issue is repentance while there is still time (2 Pet 3:8-13). We live between the resurrection of Jesus and his final return—in the days of those waiting for the dissolution and renewal of all things. In that context, the apostles taught the believers by the Spirit of Christ what it meant to live the Christian life. That life is still the life required of a true disciple today. And it will be the life required of every disciple until the return of our Lord.

What we mean when we say that the preacher must be a biblical theologian is nothing more and nothing less than that he must read the Bible biblically. At the heart of biblical preaching is not the question of interpretation but rather the question of faith. God's voice is heard by those willing to obey him on his terms, not by those with the most up-to-date theories about meaning. There is no biblical expectation that people on the last day will be able to accuse God of being too hard to understand, or that their cultural situation will allow them to blame God for their lack of knowledge and obedience. The scriptural expectation is that God's perfect judgement will be enacted, and acknowledged as righteous by all. All people will be held to account for knowing the will of God and failing to do it (Rom 1:18-32).

Once we understand the progressive nature of revelation and the fulfilment of all the promises of God in Christ Jesus, we are in a position to read the Bible as God wants it to be read. And so the more we work at understanding the whole Bible in the light of Christ and understanding Christ in the light of the whole Bible—that is, the more we work on our biblical theology—the more faithfully we will preach God's word.

A good preacher will be a good biblical theologian. He will read the Bible as a book about Jesus. On this basis alone can the preacher hope to speak God's very words to a world that needs to hear them.

LET'S SUMMARIZE BRIEFLY. Every sermon is like an arrow. It is to be carefully crafted by the preacher in order to deliver the arrowhead into the heart of the hearer. In order for the arrow to fly straight and true, it must be fitted with the right feathers. It must be prepared by examining the passage carefully in light of the whole of God's biblical revelation. Preachers can only do this well by self-consciously growing in their doctrine. We must work at letting our picture of God and his world be shaped by God's word, and at the same time we must read that word in light of the picture we have already gained from it.

To put it another way: the 'simple Bible preacher' is in fact the faithfully self-conscious biblical and systematic theologian.

The moral of the story: choose your feathers wisely.

Chapter 5

The archer and the target

Dave exhaled small mushroom clouds with each quiet breath. Something was moving—about 150 yards up the valley—through the dim half-glow of the looming dawn. It was the end of many months of planning and learning.

When Dave moved into the area from out of state, it hadn't taken long to meet the bow-hunting locals. Apparently it was just what you did if you lived in this part of the world. He'd sat and listened to their stories and started asking questions. He'd felt the adrenalin buzz as he heard a new mate retell the story of felling his first whitetail buck. He'd spent hours trying, failing, and then trying again to fashion his own arrows. He'd studied aerial photos in conjunction with topographic maps to master the lie of the land so that he could find the ideal spot to hunt from. He'd chosen his stand carefully and he'd been there, waiting stiffly in the autumn chill, for so long that it felt like his knees might never bend again.

But it was about to be worth it. He was sure of it now. Whatever it was, was coming closer. He began to discern the faint grey silhouette of the young buck against the pallid backdrop of snow-tainted underbrush. He wasn't huge, but he wasn't small either—maybe 180lbs—a fine first bag. Slowly. Silently. Dave picked up the bow and set the arrow on the string. He trained his sight on the approaching buck and tried to settle his breathing.

Keep coming. Keep coming.

He drew the bow, feeling the weight of the string press almost painfully into his fingertips. Then he waited as eternity ticked by with determined slowness. The itch above his left eye grew in his mind until it was like a thousand tiny insects gnawing at the surface of his skin. But still he waited—waited—for the perfect moment.

In one deft movement, he let the arrow fly. Swiftly. Silently. Dreadfully.

He missed by a country mile. There was one more thing he needed to know—how to fire a bow.

It is, of course, a rather silly illustration—as if someone would go to all of that effort without having learned the basics of actually being able to fire the arrows he'd made. But it raises an important question. In the world of archery, no matter how good the arrows are, there is always the matter of the archer. Without a skilled archer, even the most perfect arrows end up being useless. Is this the case with preaching?

We have already seen that regeneration and obedience are essential for knowing and understanding God's word, and that the character and heart of the preacher are important. But what of his speaking skills? Will the perfect sermon fall dead on the lips of the unskilled communicator? What part does the preacher and his preaching play in the process of delivering the word of God?

It's time for another diagram.[10]

---

10. 'Common grace' in the diagram is a theological term referring to the generous blessings and gifts of God we experience simply by virtue of being God's creatures and living in God's good world, whether we are God's people or not—for example, "he makes his sun rise on the evil and on the good" (Matt 5:45).

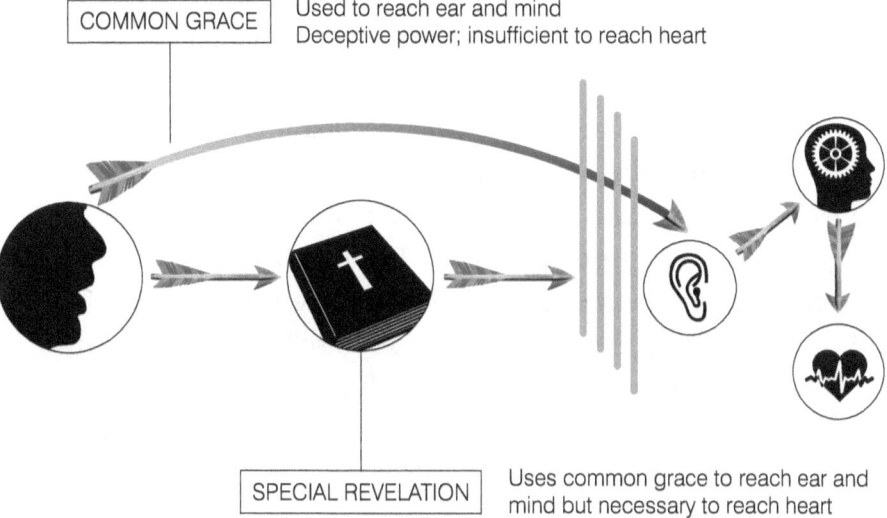

The purpose of the diagram is to describe the process of preaching. It's a simple and yet miraculous process, in which the speaker announces the very words of God to the listener. But the aim is not that the listener might acknowledge the receipt of the soundwaves. Rather, we pray that God's words would penetrate the minds of the hearers, and through their minds their hearts.

Why the heart? Not because it is the seat of our emotions—that is a very modern understanding of the heart—but because biblically the heart is the core of the human being, the centre of our will and affections. The heart is involved in our thinking and our feeling. But it is more than both of these. The heart represents who we are—what we love and long for. And the aim of preaching is to change the heart so that it loves what God loves and hates what God hates. In the process, the entire life of the hearer is transformed into the likeness of Christ.

How, then, do the words that the preacher speaks enter the ear, the mind and the heart of the hearer? It is a complex process that involves a number of obstacles. The first involves the stance of the listener. In the diagram, the ear of the hearer is turned away from the preacher. The most profound barrier in the process of preaching is the sinful nature of human beings. As sinners, we do not long to listen to God. Indeed, we would rather listen to the weekend sports results, the latest gossip or even the most inane trivia than listen to what God has to say.

But this isn't the only difficulty. The diagram depicts a whole set of barriers between the speaker and the listener. Some of these have been established by God himself. For example, in his judgement on humanity, God dispersed human beings over the face of the earth and confused their languages (Gen 11:9). God reinforced our self-reliant disobedience as part of his judgement by making human relationships more difficult. This has led to friction in our relationships with God and each other ever since. Throughout the Scriptures, this process of rebellion and judgement is a reinforcing cycle—explained most clearly in Romans 1 where idolatrous rejection of God leads to hearts hardened by God, which in turn leads to further rejection (also see 2 Thess 2:9-12).

Part of the result of this process is a world in which there are many barriers to communication. These barriers range from profound to almost inconsequential. They include things like language and personal relationships—you may choose to ignore everything the preacher says because for some reason you don't like him, or you may choose to listen to everything he says because you really like him, both of which can be barriers to the truth. It may be as simple as present comfort levels—people may be too cold, too tired or too hungry to be able to listen. Or it may be the mundane realities of communication—the PA system is playing up and people can't actually hear what we are saying.

It's important that we do not over-spiritualize or demythologize any of these realities. People may be too cold and hungry for any number of reasons. They might be hungry because they got up too late to eat breakfast before church. They may be cold because they have no money for clothes, or because the weather suddenly turned sour and they didn't bring their jacket. It may be that they've decided not to eat because they are Muslim and it's Ramadan. Some of these issues are simply a result of living in this created but fallen order; others may be the result of spiritual blindness. Sometimes the PA system doesn't work properly because it's being run by inept people, and sometimes it's because Satan doesn't want people to hear what is being said. And quite possibly, it could be both of these things at the same time.

The point is not that we need to develop greater discernment but that communication happens in a created context for human beings—a context that is scarred by sin and affected by the limitations of being human. To express this theologically: part of the preacher's job is to be aware that any act of preaching involves communicating God's special revelation in the context of God's created order.

Being aware of, and responding to, the created nature of our hearers is not faithlessness, nor is it a descent into human methodology. Good preachers will ensure that the PA system is working well, that the physical environment is neither too hot nor too cold (where we can have any influence over such things), and that people's basic welfare is taken care of. We are just being foolish if we preach for two hours to a group of hungry, tired, cold people and then disparage them for their spiritual hard-heartedness when they don't remember everything we just said!

But of course, our createdness extends beyond the environment and physical comfort of the hearer. Some of the barriers are a subtle combination of human sinfulness and created reality. If the preacher smiles and makes people laugh, they are more likely to listen. If the preacher is earnest or flippant, it will affect the way that hearers hear. What is more, it is impossible to be all things to all people at one and the same moment. What is playful and enjoyable for some may be irreverent or frivolous for others.

Nevertheless, preachers should try as much as possible to understand the culture of their audience and to preach in a way that is appropriate. This will extend from the kind of humour we employ (or choose not to employ) to the kind of clothing that we choose to wear. It is all part of breaking down the barriers that might keep our listeners from hearing what is said.

Another aspect of barrier removal involves saying things that aren't contrary to, but are certainly apart from, the word of God. For example, this book aims to communicate the word of God. And at times, particularly in those places where the text of Scripture is quoted, that aim is obvious. But we have also spoken about all sorts of things that aren't the word of God. The arrow illustration is not the word of God. And yet it aims to communicate God's truths. We must remember that in God's world, the truth always belongs to God and lies always belong to Satan. Because of common grace it is possible for the unbeliever to observe God's world and understand some truths. And it is possible to appeal to our common human experience in order for communication to take place. All preaching involves communicating God's life-giving special revelation through the often mundane gifts of common grace.

Paul, for example, appeals to the common knowledge of creation as he preaches in Lystra (Acts 14:15-17). Later in Acts, he appeals to the commonly available knowledge of the events of Jesus (Acts 26:26). Jesus uses his hearers' knowledge of the "birds of the air" and the "lilies of the field" in his teaching about the kingdom (Matt 6:25-34).

To return to our diagram, good preaching acknowledges the significance of living in the created order that God has given to all by his common grace. We speak as human beings to other human beings in God's world. Godly wisdom will seek to be aware of the whole process of communication and not just the accuracy of our words. From the language spoken to the vocabulary chosen, and from the structure of the talk to the eye-contact that we make, it is all part of the communication process. In these things, the preacher matters. Some preachers are better at these things than others, but everyone who preaches should seek to grow in them, so that what we say may be intelligible to those who hear (1 Cor 14:6-12).

Speaking special revelation to a created world

However, we need to acknowledge the significant tension involved in this discussion. Because we live in God's creation, the preacher (just like the archer) matters in delivering the sermon. And yet common grace gifts of charm and persuasion—and even an Einstein-like grasp of general revelation—will never achieve our ultimate goal of seeing people live in relationship with God as their saviour and lord. Common grace may get us to the ear and even the mind of the hearer, but without the revealed truth of God implanted by the illumination of the Spirit, the heart will never be changed.

The challenge is twofold. On the one hand we must resist being seduced by the promise of savvy communication, and on the other we must not resort to using 'special revelation' as an excuse for our own ineptitude.

In our holy longing to see more people knowing God (and in our less-noble desire to be more popular), we are seduced into preaching what people want to hear. But more people listening, more people talking excitedly about how interesting the preacher was, and more people inviting their friends back next time— these are not necessarily the test of good preaching. Visible results are deeply deceptive for the preacher of God's word.

Preaching is a week-in, week-out, year-in, year-out task that is never fully completed on this side of the heavenly rest. This can be discouraging at times. And it is only natural, given the hard work required in preparation and delivery, that we desire to see the fruits of our labour. But that desire is seductively deceptive.

We long to hear people say, "He's a great preacher". But we forget that what they are really saying is: "He's a funny guy who possesses natural comedic timing and a winsome smile". If we are preaching for the sake of God's honour, then we will long for our hearers to say, "Jesus is a great saviour" not "He is a great preacher".

But our desire to guard ourselves from the deep deceits of our own hearts can lead to the opposite folly. Many years ago now, a number of very clever students at a university were converted to Christ and then became involved in a sect. According to the sect, the only way that people could be converted was to hear the pure word of God. And according to them, the pure word of God was contained only in the King James Version.

Their method of evangelism was therefore to walk around the university campus wearing sandwich boards printed with verses from the King James Bible. They refused to engage people in conversation because they were fearful of distorting the word of God. To mingle God's words with merely human words would be to distort and ultimately destroy them. So they simply walked around the campus with sandwich boards inscribed with biblical texts.

This is plainly a denial of God as our creator and our nature as image-bearers. If they really believed in their message, they should have carried sandwich boards written in the original Greek and Hebrew—which would have been even more 'pure' and just as useful!

Even the process of translation is an acknowledgement of common grace and the created order. The Christian translator will translate more sensitively and accurately than the non-Christian. But the trained non-Christian will translate the Bible better than the Christian with only rudimentary knowledge of the original languages. Common grace is a part of all communication. It's the way God made us.

No level of commitment to the clarity, perspicuity, authority, divinity and power of special revelation can avoid the need to pay attention to our created nature. Every preacher will improve their preaching by thinking hard about the use of illustrations, learning good microphone technique and practising the rhetorical arts—like learning to pause—for example. Some excellent content is being lost in the barriers around human ears. Transforming truth needs to be spoken in such a way that it does not send the hearer to sleep.

But equally, intoxication with the power of communication techniques and disillusionment at the hard-heartedness of our hearers should not lead us to become joke-tellers and motivational speakers. If we find ourselves beholden to the emotional power of anecdotes rather than prayerfully seeking the life-changing work of God's word in people's hearts, then we have ceased to be what God calls on us to be—faithful speakers of his life-changing truth who preach his word in season and out of season, with complete patience (2 Tim 4:2).

Understanding the target

So far in this chapter, we've been speaking about the part that the archer plays in the world of archery. But if our aim is to communicate God's special revelation in the context of created reality, the process of communication is about more than just the communicator. It's also about the audience. Here the inherent weaknesses of the archery illustration become apparent. If the preacher is the archer then what should we call the congregation? Words like prey, quarry and victim leave a certain something to be desired!

Perhaps we should talk about the 'target audience'. If we remember that the arrows we fire are the arrows of God's word, designed to pierce every one of us and change our hearts for our good and God's glory, then perhaps target isn't such a terrible description. But the big question is: what does it mean to understand your target?

Following the work of Donald MacGavran and the 'School of World Missions' in the middle of last century, sociological issues have found a permanent home in the fields of church growth and missiology. The modern pastor is constantly being encouraged to understand everything about their sheep—from what they eat for breakfast to how they spend their spare time. It's supposed to make our preaching relevant. But it's a classic case of putting the cart before the sheep (to mangle the metaphor).

The assumption has been made that we will understand the sheep better by listening to them rather than listening to their creator. But nothing could be further from the truth. As well-intentioned as the desire to become more relevant might be, it flows from a false assessment of the human condition. If our problem as human beings is that we lack a sense of worth and personal fulfilment, then by all means let the surveys and sociology roll on. But if God's diagnosis is right—if we are sinful creatures out of communion with our creator and destined for judgement, whose entire understanding of the world has been warped by our disobedience—then sociological research misses the point.

If we are even half as sinful as God tells us we are, we cannot be trusted to diagnose our own problems, let alone discover the required solutions. That is why our best target research is done in the Scriptures. The Bible tells us what people are like. God's word provides the glasses through which we most clearly perceive the needs of those we preach to. The Bible grants us the spiritual insight to see the half-hearted, self-obsessed, self-deceived, God-rejecting, neighbour-coveting hearts of our ourselves and our hearers. And the Scriptures also provide us with the only possible solution—the gospel of Jesus.

We are returning to a point we have made already: the Bible does not need to be made relevant. Just as the first Christians didn't need to learn the intricacies of the Jewish culture in order to read Deuteronomy as their book, so we do not need to wear sandals and tunics to make sense of a New Testament written two millennia ago. The Bible is relevant to us because it addresses us, as we are, about the problems that most desperately plague us, and it provides God's own remedy for our maladies.

But as we have already seen in this chapter, listening to God's word and accepting his diagnosis of our condition does not require ignoring created reality. On the contrary, the gospel addresses us as real people living in God's created order. You don't have to go far in the Scriptures to find the gospel challenging the reality of our sex-obsessed society, or to hear God talking about how to love and serve our neighbours, or to find heavenly wisdom for raising our children.

One of our mistakes is that we too readily accept the old adage "too heavenly minded to be any earthly use". We give in too quickly when the world tells us that the Bible is old and out of date. If we are really reading and preaching God's word, then it will address us in all of our life.

That is why we would be foolish to ignore the common human experience of living in creation. God created the world in wisdom, and even in our sinfulness we can see and observe some of the ways in which the created world works. For example, say you are running a university mission, and you want to put on an event to gather the students together so that you could talk to them about Jesus. What sort of event should it be? You don't have to be a genius to figure out that a colouring-in contest might not be very effective. That's not a spiritual or moral judgement; it's a matter of observation, experience and wisdom. Knowing the gospel is therefore not an excuse for poor observation skills or lack of wisdom.

Paul uses such wisdom in 2 Timothy 2:1-7. He illustrates the point he is making to Timothy by pointing to the single-minded soldier, and the athlete who competes according to the rules, and the hard-working farmer who gets the first share of the crops. The characteristics of these three sorts of 'faithful workers' are matters of common observation and wisdom.

Here again the challenge of preaching special revelation in the context of created reality raises questions that every preacher needs to be willing to ask of themselves and answer honestly.

For example, if your congregation is finding your preaching boring or wide of the mark, it could indicate any one of a number of things. Perhaps your sermons are incoherent or failing to communicate the riches and wonder of God's truth. Maybe your illustrations are tangential, or perhaps you use too many clichés and end up boring people. If this is the case, then no amount of railing against your audience's lack of spirituality will help you. Ask some trusted friends to genuinely assess your preaching, and be willing to listen to what they have to say.

Then again, it may be that you are preaching clearly and powerfully about the life-giving work of Jesus, but your congregation is full of traditional religionists who are not converted and who don't want to hear the truth. In this case, you have no choice but to keep struggling to speak the truth that people don't want to hear.

These are not easy questions to face. They involve making a wise and sober assessment of ourselves and the people that God has given us to love. This is yet another reason why our exposition of the Bible needs to be *prayerful*. We need to pray for God's wisdom to understand our situation from the perspective of God's truth.

To put it simply, we must observe our target audience carefully through the glasses of God's word, always remembering that we are also one of the targets.

Another Dave

Dave exhaled small mushroom clouds with each quiet breath. The congregation huddled together for warmth on the cold autumn morning. It was the culmination of years of study and planning, and another small step in the lifelong work of understanding the target and prayerfully seeking to be God's preacher. He had met during the week with George, who became a Christian two months ago. He'd sat and listened while Rachel told him about the ongoing agony of post-natal depression at the mid-week Mums and Tots group. And he'd eked out some oh-so-precious time to read and re-read the Bible and to craft his arrow.

He climbed into the pulpit, picked up the Bible and set the arrow on the string. He trained his sight on the silent crowd who had gathered, and tried to settle his breathing, praying that God would change people this morning. He drew the bow, feeling the weight of the string press almost painfully into his fingertips and opened his mouth and began to speak. In the next thirty minutes he let fly the arrow of God's word.

It was strange watching that arrow do its work. In God's kindness, the arrow flew straight and true at the hearts of each person there. At some ribs, the arrow stopped abruptly, as if repelled by some unseen armour hidden under the skin, and dropped harmlessly to the floor. But in others, the arrow penetrated deeply and drew blood, and Dave could see the joy in their faces.

As the sermon ended, Dave gave thanks to God. Mission accomplished for another week. Well, at least until morning tea, when he was hoping to fire some more arrows.

BECAUSE DAVE KNOWS GOD and because he understands the power of his word, he has spent a lifetime studying the word and prayerfully seeking to preach it and obey it. And because he understands what God has to say about living in creation, he has spent time listening to and understanding his people, in order to faithfully speak the eternal life-giving word of God.

Does the preacher matter? Of course. Do the Scriptures tell us everything we need to hear to live as God's people in his world? Absolutely. Does Dave need to keep listening to his congregation? Definitely. Will God do his work according to his sovereign will? He will!

Chapter 6

To those God has given me to love

> *My aim is to preach the gospel by prayerfully expounding the Bible to the people God has given me to love.*

So far we have seen why our aim must be to preach the gospel, and why the gospel is most faithfully preached by prayerfully expounding the Bible. We have looked carefully at what it means to expound the Scriptures and we have thought about how this all occurs in the context of created reality. But there is one vital part of the mission statement that we have not yet considered—that preaching occurs in the context of God's call to love people.

Why should we spend so much time seeking to understand God's word truly? Why should we spend years honing our craft and learning to speak wisely and well in light of the culture that we live in? Why will we preach the gospel when people want to hear it and when they do not? The biblical answer is love. As Paul puts it:

> ... the love of Christ controls us, because we have concluded this: that one has died for all, therefore all have died; and he died for all, that those who live might no longer live for themselves but for him who for their sake died and was raised.

> From now on, therefore, we regard no-one according
> to the flesh. Even though we once regarded Christ
> according to the flesh, we regard him thus no longer.
> (2 Cor 5:14-16)

Those who know the love of Christ can no longer see the world in the same way. Where once they looked at Jesus and saw folly, now they look at him and see life and love personified. When we come to Christ, our whole world view is changed. We regard Christ in a totally new way and as a result we regard *people* in a totally new way. People do not exist to be used or abused. They are not obstacles to be overcome or competitors to be vanquished. They are image-bearers to be loved. Because we live for Christ, we live for the sake of others.

That was the motivation that led the apostle Paul to go hungry and cold, to be shipwrecked and beaten, and to be left for dead on the side of the road after being stoned—it was all so that he could preach the gospel to a world that needed to know God. It sounds like the outrageous life of a dedicated and holy few. But biblically it ought to be the way of life for all Christians.

In 1 Corinthians 8-10, the apostle Paul speaks of his rights in the gospel. He concludes that those who understand the gospel are not ultimately concerned with rights but with freedom expressed in love. Jesus Christ frees us from selfishness to serve him. That is why Paul seeks to do uncomfortable things for others. He concludes with these remarkable words:

> So, whether you eat or drink, or whatever you do, do all
> to the glory of God. Give no offense to Jews or to Greeks
> or to the church of God, just as I try to please everyone
> in everything I do, not seeking my own advantage, but
> that of many, that they may be saved.
>
> Be imitators of me, as I am of Christ. (1 Cor 10:31-11:1)

Paul desires to use his freedom to bring the message of Jesus to others, and so to bring glory to God. And this is the pattern that he lays down for all believers: "Be imitators of me, as I am of Christ". As the pattern of life for all of God's people, it is to be the pattern of life in particular for those who preach and teach his word. We are to preach the gospel by prayerfully expounding the Bible to *the people God has given us to love*! The preacher who speaks without love is nothing but a clanging gong.

What does this love look like? 1 Thessalonians 1-2 contains one of the clearest and most moving examples in the New Testament. According to Acts, Paul's stay in Thessalonica was brief—a matter of weeks rather than months. He came, he preached the gospel, people were converted, and the city descended into uproar (Acts 17:1-10). Paul was smuggled out of the city at nightfall and sent on his way. A fledgling church was formed, but their future was in the balance. What would happen to those who had become Christians in the face of such persecution?

Paul's first letter to the Thessalonians is a message of encouragement to those following Christ and suffering for it. It is a letter of assurance. Paul wants the Thessalonians to know that their suffering, far from indicating God's disfavour, is a sign of their genuine conversion. He tells them that he knows that they have been chosen by God "because our gospel came to you not only in word, but also in power and in the Holy Spirit and with full conviction" (1 Thess 1:5). How did Paul know that the gospel came by the power of the Holy Spirit? It was because they embraced the gospel despite the suffering that it brought: "And you became imitators of us and of the Lord, for you received the word in much affliction, with the joy of the Holy Spirit, so that you became an example to all the believers in Macedonia and in Achaia" (1 Thess 1:6-7).

Paul encouraged the Thessalonians by reminding them of the authenticity of his gospel and apostleship. How was his genuine apostleship displayed? In his life. He refused to use flattery; he declined the opportunity to seek his own glory; he did not seek to make demands on the Thessalonians, but was gentle, "like a nursing mother taking care of her own children" (1 Thess 2:7).

There may be no greater example of tenderness in our world than the gentle care of a mother for her newborn infant—the way she touches her baby; the way she wraps her son or daughter to keep out the cold; the way she cuddles and coos, comforts and caresses and sings sweetly when sleep will not come. It is an image of care and joy, of grace and concern—an image of love. It is the kind of love Paul had for the Thessalonians.

It was not a cheap love that just mouths the words. It is easy to say, "I love you". But Paul's love was like the love of our Lord Jesus—a love shown in action. Paul laboured, working night and day, in order not to burden the Thessalonians. He didn't want the gospel being misheard because he demanded his livelihood from those that he preached to. He lived amongst them. He provided for his own needs, and he sought to share his life with those that he brought Jesus to.

This is one of the most strikingly personal parts of the whole Bible. Paul's concern for his people pours out and he cannot help himself. "Being affectionately desirous of you, we were ready to share with you not only the gospel of God but also our own selves, because you had become very dear to us" (1 Thess 2:8). Paul lived and served and preached to the people that God had given him to love. And his love was displayed in the details of his life.

This is one of the reasons that internet ministry will never replace true pastoral ministry. Of course it is possible, and good, to be blessed by hearing faithful biblical teaching from other parts of the world. But it is not the same thing as living together as God's gathered people. The pastor who lives with his people laughs with them and cries with them; he shares the joys and sorrows of this broken but God-given life. He learns to love his people. And they learn to love him.

Paul's ministry grew from the love that he had learned from Christ. And so like a father with his children, he exhorted each one of them and encouraged them and charged them to walk in a manner worthy of God, who called them into his own kingdom and glory (1 Thess 2:11-12). Paul preached both in public and in private. He exhorted each one (cf. Acts 20:18-21). Paul got to know his people and he spoke the truth to them, because love compelled him to tell them about the God who calls all to share his kingdom and his glory.

Paul had come to understand God's love for the world. He could do nothing else except long for people to know Jesus. And so he lived faithfully and obediently amongst the Thessalonians, and he spoke God's word to them.

But Paul's love for these people extended beyond the time he spent with them. Paul cared so deeply, that when he was forced to leave Thessalonica, his concern did not cease.

> But since we were torn away from you, brothers, for a short time, in person not in heart, we endeavoured the more eagerly and with great desire to see you face to face, because we wanted to come to you—I, Paul, again and again—but Satan hindered us. For what is our hope or joy or crown of boasting before our Lord Jesus at his coming? Is it not you? For you are our glory and joy.
> (1 Thess 2:17-20)

Because Paul loved the Thessalonians, he longed for them to remain steadfast in Christ. Their salvation was the goal of his ministry. They were the crowning joy of his ministry. Nothing would be better than to stand with them in the presence of Jesus at his return. And so when he could not minister to them personally, he sent Timothy to do what he could not do.

> Therefore when we could bear it no longer, we were willing to be left behind at Athens alone, and we sent Timothy, our brother and God's coworker in the gospel of Christ, to establish and exhort you in your faith, that no-one be moved by these afflictions. (1 Thess 3:1-3)

Paul was willing to relinquish one of his precious fellow workers for the sake of seeing the Thessalonians persevering in their faith. Listen one last time to the place that the Thessalonians held in Paul's affections:

> But now that Timothy has come to us from you, and has brought us the good news of your faith and love and reported that you always remember us kindly and long to see us, as we long to see you—for this reason, brothers, in all our distress and affliction we have been comforted about you through your faith. For now we live, if you are standing fast in the Lord. For what thanksgiving can we return to God for you, for all the joy that we feel for your sake before our God, as we pray most earnestly night and day that we may see you face to face and supply what is lacking in your faith? (1 Thess 3:6-10)

Paul's love for people—the love that drove him to serve them with the gospel—is not a technique. It's not something that you can learn in three simple steps. It's not a management strategy designed to increase your number of conversions. People will easily see through such falsehood. Paul's love was a genuine affection for people—an affection that grew in him through knowing God's love for his world.

How will this love grow in us? It will grow as we read and

see God's heart revealed in the gospel. It will grow as God's Spirit works in us so that we imitate Paul as he imitates Christ. True biblical preaching will flow from genuine love, and genuine love will be grown by true biblical preaching.

> In this is love, not that we have loved God but that he loved us and sent his Son to be the propitiation for our sins. Beloved, if God so loved us, we also ought to love one another. No-one has ever seen God; if we love one another, God abides in us and his love is perfected in us. (1 John 4:10-12)

Chapter 7

The risks the preacher takes

Some professions are inherently dangerous. Soldiers will be shot at occasionally. Racing drivers shouldn't be surprised when various parts of their anatomy are crushed in spectacular accidents. Hunters sometimes end up as the hunted. And gospel preachers should expect to suffer. Jesus told us it would be so.

> "If the world hates you, know that it has hated me before it hated you. If you were of the world, the world would love you as its own; but because you are not of the world, but I chose you out of the world, therefore the world hates you. Remember the word that I said to you: 'A servant is not greater than his master'. If they persecuted me, they will also persecute you." (John 15:18-20)

There is one last biblical promise that every preacher must be aware of. "Indeed, all who desire to live a godly life in Christ Jesus will be persecuted" (2 Tim 3:12).

Paul doesn't speak like this because he is a pessimist, or because he has a depressive outlook on life, but because he believes it is one of the promises of God in the gospel. Just as glory followed suffering for the Messiah, so glory will follow suffering for his servants. In the present evil age in which we live, those who seek to preach the truth and live for righteousness will always suffer.

That's why this book would be incomplete without the reminder that the preacher's vocation will be marked by suffering. Here are seven reasons that we should not expect to be loved for preaching the gospel by faithfully expounding the Bible.

1. Preachers are absolutists in an age of relativism

The worst offence in today's society is to impose your views upon others. Ours is an 'I'm OK, you're OK' age where evangelism is equivalent to brain-washing. The world longs for peace and unity, and so it calls on everyone to respect each other's views. Unfortunately, relativism has been the result. The only sure way to peace is to pretend that there is no such thing as truth, because only then can you avoid the problem of somebody being upset because they are wrong. The modern western world cannot stand disagreement or division.

But this isn't an exclusively modern emphasis. Pilate was one of the great relativists of his age. He could see no difference between releasing Barabbas on one hand or Jesus on the other. It didn't matter that one was a murderer and the other was entirely innocent—as long as the peace was kept. If the people were happy, Pilate was happy, regardless of the truth. After all, what is truth (see John 18:38)?

That's why Christian preaching has always been unpopular, because it insists that there are right and wrong ideas about life. When we say that it is universally true that God can only be known through Jesus Christ, we put every religious relativist offside. This is a risk that a preacher must take.

2. Preachers call for repentance

Not only do we declare what we believe to be universally true, but we also claim that our listeners need to change. We get personal. We call for sinners to change their lives; to turn towards God and away from what is wrong.

It is hard to call for repentance in a genteel fashion. Suggesting to someone that his or her life is odious to God is hardly the stuff of after-dinner conversation. Preaching the gospel can mean social death. But the faithful preacher cannot therefore refuse to act as the watchman. God calls on us to announce the coming judgement.

This is not an excuse to justify personal rudeness or unnecessary offence. If we are going to exhort people to repentance we should approach the task with humility and discernment, knowing that we are also speaking to ourselves. It is not the preacher who has the power to condemn, but the message he preaches.

Even so, calling people to repentance, and accepting the consequences, is another risk that a preacher must take.

3. Preachers risk offending the powerful

People who are powerful often don't appreciate their power, and regularly refuse to accept challenges levelled at their lives. Unrecognized power is like a set of blinkers that makes true self-understanding very difficult. Gospel preaching, by its very nature, challenges everyone, from the greatest to the least. Preachers who preach God's word are going to put powerful noses out of joint. When powerful people are attacked by our preaching, and they sense their power waning, they may go to any lengths to regain it.

We tend to take our power as preachers for granted—until it is taken away from us. Ask any retired preacher and he will tell you about the frustration of not being allowed regularly into the pulpit. But we spend most of our time frustrated with the limitations of our power rather than noticing its strength.

4. Popular prophets are either dead or foreigners

After a dud sermon, many a desperate preacher finds solace in Jesus' words in Luke 4:24: "Truly I say to you, no prophet is acceptable in his hometown". Everyone loves a prophet, as long as he is either well dead and therefore idealized to the point of fantasy, or a foreign 'treasure' whom no-one really understands anyway.

Jesus' words in Matthew 23 tell us more about people's attitudes towards prophets:

> "Woe to you, scribes and Pharisees, hypocrites! For you build the tombs of the prophets and decorate the monuments of the righteous, saying, 'If we had lived in the days of our fathers, we would not have taken part with them in shedding the blood of the prophets'. Thus you witness against yourselves that you are sons of those who murdered the prophets. Fill up, then, the measure of your fathers." (Matt 23:29-32)

Although they would not align themselves with the message of the prophets, the Jewish leaders still venerated them, happily calling them 'forefathers'.

Religious authorities have a history of persecuting prophets. In 1660, the Anglican authorities sent John Bunyan to prison for 12 years; now, he's a Protestant saint. The story is similar for Wesley, Simeon and Whitefield. All are praised today as great leaders and visionaries, but in their time they were persecuted by the established church. That is a preacher's lot. All preachers risk unpopularity and persecution, from the godless as well as from the religious authorities.

Strangely enough, the reverse situation is also true. It is

somewhat trendy to talk about a leader as a 'prophetic voice'. But if the gurus of current religious fashion consider us 'prophetic', chances are we are not saying anything other than what they want to hear. If you earn that epithet, ask yourself whether you are bowing to the pressures of current fads and compromising the truth.

5. People want to catch us out

Jesus experienced the hypocrisy of the Pharisees when they tried to trap him over a question of financial loyalty (Mark 12:13ff). Jesus' reply was brilliant. He turned the tables on his accusers and amazed them with the truth.

In the 21st century, hypocrites who are opposed to God's word are still trying to catch preachers in their words. These days, they are assisted in their task by the invention of audio recordings, printing presses, and most significant of all, the internet. Our opponents are always able to pore over our words in search of dirt.

Such people are hypocrites, because they appear to be listening but they are not. They are not listening to what we are saying for its own value; rather, their only intent is to dredge up material by which to condemn us. They may quote us out of context, or focus upon trivial issues in order to tarnish our reputations, or pose loaded questions to catch us out. All this goes with the preacher's territory.

6. Preachers risk being misunderstood

People tend to have extreme reactions to anything a preacher states that goes against the norm. If we are challenging careerism, they will hear us denying that work has any value. If we are challenging the western pattern of romance, they will hear us saying you should choose your marriage partner out of a hat. If we are challenging British imperialism, they will hear that we are against missionary work. If we are challenging unbiblical uses of ecclesiastical power, they will hear that we are disloyal to our denominations.

If we are being misunderstood, it is our responsibility to become better communicators. However, every preacher lives with the knowledge that he cannot reach all of his listeners all of the time. The flexibility and ambiguity of language, along with the inflexibility and fixed mindset of some hearers, means that preachers are bound to be misunderstood.

Jesus was regularly misunderstood. Paul was wilfully misunderstood by those who wanted to make his life difficult. You may find your name used to support ideas that are distortions of what you really think. And the bigger your audience and the more remote your relationship with them, the more chance you have of being misrepresented.

Preachers must learn not to spend their entire lives trying to protect their reputation. It is impossible.

7. Preachers avoid balance[11]

It may seem strange to suggest that preachers should strive for anything other than balanced preaching, but we must. Balanced preaching is impossible, boring, unmotivating and ultimately unbalanced!

It is impossible because we can never say everything in a sermon. Our message is always slanted to a certain extent by what we have left unsaid. There is a time and place for balanced statements and careful constructions of Christian beliefs, but it is not when we preach.

---

11. For more on this, see appendix II: 'Preach the negative as well as the positive'.

This is not to say that we must begin preaching untruth. As we saw in chapter 3, wise gospel preaching will always preach with the whole of the gospel circle in mind. Since each part of the truth is still true, unbalanced preaching does not mean faithless preaching. But if we are constantly seeking for balance we will ultimately fail as preachers.

Balanced preaching is boring and unmotivating because it lacks the vigour to challenge people's presuppositions. People need to be taken step by step into the gospel, and to suffer the disturbing and motivating experience of having their worldly presuppositions dismantled. Balanced preaching tends to proceed too quickly to the rounded, balanced, finished product, leaving the hearer with a sense of neatness and familiarity rather than challenge.

Balanced preaching ends up being unbalanced itself, for it teaches a moderate, safe, half-hearted Christianity. The Bible doesn't call us to a 'balanced Christian life'. God calls us to have a 'madness' for God ('zeal' is the religiously acceptable word)— a madness that makes us challenge people to abandon their careers, leave their families and give up their lives to follow Christ.

Preachers are compelled, therefore, to be unbalanced. We have to confront worldly apathy and conservatism with the gospel, so that lives will be changed. In doing so, we run the risk of being offensive, unpopular, persecuted and misunderstood. Yet the risks do not negate reality. We cannot change people's lifelong presuppositions by merely mentioning them in passing. A penitent heart is one that has been battered by the truth. We are better off attacking one important point with vigour, humour and repetition than presenting a balanced and comprehensive message that causes no wounds.

Preachers are required to take a stand against religious relativism, denying the alternatives to the truth that we want to hammer home. We may, at times, have to come down on one side of a paradox. We may have to employ rhetorical hyperbole, shocking people's minds in order to reach their hearts. Jesus' outrageous remark in Luke 14:26 that his disciples must hate their families was not flippant and should not be blunted. It smashes our most treasured preconceptions in order to make room for the truth. That's what a gospel preacher does.

Preachers shine strong light into the darkest corners of people's hearts and chase out their excuses for ignoring God. We reveal their hiding places, demanding a response to what we say. We simplify the issues for people, clearing the foggy areas in which people hide from God so that they can see the decisions before them. We are called to run the risk of laying bare a heart that is blocked up with sin. It's the risk of being unbalanced. If we are committed to balanced preaching, we are denying the depth and resilience of that sin. But if we commit ourselves to the dangerous declaration of a gospel that demands response, we will see at work our zealous, attention-demanding God.

TO PUT IT SIMPLY: the preacher who runs the risk of preaching the gospel by prayerfully expounding the Bible will suffer and be persecuted. The Bible tells us to expect nothing less, but we easily forget this lesson—not least because we don't want to hear it. We want a ministry that is joyous and peaceful. We want people to shake our hands warmly at the door and tell us what a wonderful sermon it was. We want to be well-thought-of by our peers, and approved of by the world.

But that is not the path of faithfulness. If we are going to be faithful preachers of the very words of God, delivering, explaining and applying his message to the people he has given us to love, we need to be ready for those times when people don't love us back. Paul tells Timothy that all who desire to live a godly life will be persecuted (2 Tim 3:12), before going on to charge him in the most solemn terms not to be deflected from his faithfulness to the God-breathed word of the Scriptures:

> I charge you in the presence of God and of Christ Jesus, who is to judge the living and the dead, and by his appearing and his kingdom: preach the word; be ready in season and out of season; reprove, rebuke, and exhort, with complete patience and teaching. For the time is coming when people will not endure sound teaching, but having itching ears they will accumulate for themselves teachers to suit their own passions, and will turn away from listening to the truth and wander off into myths. As for you, always be sober-minded, endure suffering, do the work of an evangelist, fulfil your ministry. (2 Tim 4:1-5)

Faithfulness to the very words of God requires the humility to trust that what God says in his Scripture is more important for your congregation to hear than what *they* think they need to hear, and what *you* think they need to hear. It requires the humility to trust that explaining and expounding the Scriptures, the Scripture's way, will be more valuable in changing lives from worse to better than to answer the questions that are on everybody's lips.

This sort of faithfulness will inevitably lead to difficulty, conflict, suffering and persecution. It did for Timothy, for Paul, and of course for Jesus himself. If you aren't being persecuted, then perhaps it is time to look again at your preaching, and ask why.

But this sort of faithfulness also inevitably leads to joy: the joy of seeing people changed through the miraculous work of God's Spirit, as he applies the word to people's hearts; the joy of being counted worthy like the apostles to suffer for the Name

(Acts 5:41); and the joy that awaits us when we have finished the struggle and stand before our king. Immediately following his stirring charge to Timothy to preach the word, Paul puts it like this:

> For I am already being poured out as a drink offering, and the time of my departure has come. I have fought the good fight, I have finished the race, I have kept the faith. Henceforth there is laid up for me the crown of righteousness, which the Lord, the righteous judge, will award to me on that Day, and not only to me but also to all who have loved his appearing. (2 Tim 4:6-8)

May this faithfulness and this joy be yours in abundance.

Appendices

The three essays by Phillip reproduced in the following appendices share two characteristics. None of them quite fitted into the logic of the main body of the book, and yet they were all too good to leave on the editing room floor.

The first of them ('The strategy of God') discusses the place of preaching within the larger activity of Christian ministry, with all its demands and challenges. For example, how does preaching relate to the important task of personal discipling and training? (Or to put it another way: How does *The Archer and the Arrow* relate to *The Trellis and the Vine?*)[12]

The essay proposes that some aspects of Christian ministry and church life are given and inflexible—they are part of God's strategy and we have no right to change them. Other aspects are more 'tactical', and can flex and change according to circumstances. The trick, of course, is knowing which is which.

The second essay ('Preach the negative as well as the positive') discusses in more detail an issue raised at various points in the book—namely, that faithfully preaching the text in front of us in the Bible will at times require the courage to be negative and critical.

The third essay contains a series of tips and suggestions aimed especially at novice preachers.

PG

---

12. Col Marshall and Tony Payne's excellent book on why people ministry matters more than structures and programs. Also by Matthias Media—see page 151 for details.

Appendix I

The strategy of God

Many years ago, I was trained to teach and preach by expounding the Scriptures. I am very thankful to those who taught me this (Broughton Knox chief among them). So from the outset in ministry, I set about just working my way through the Scriptures, expounding each passage as it came up. After a time, I found myself in 1 Corinthians 8-10, and the more I prepared it, the more my heart sank. I thought to myself, "What am I supposed to do with this? Food offered to idols? Nobody offers food to idols in Australia, other than the idol of our own belly—to which we offer food reverently, often and in huge quantities. Just how am I supposed to preach on this?" It was a subject I would never have thought of preaching on, nor one that I thought was even remotely relevant to my congregation.

All the same, I did what I had been trained to do, and kept preaching through 1 Corinthians 8-10. As I did so, I became conscious of the fact that about a quarter of the congregation were Chinese and that most of them had come from families who offer food to idols constantly—in little shrines in the corner of the lounge room. For them, it was not an abstract or irrelevant issue; it was a pressing dilemma. Now that I am Christian, do I bow to the ancestors or not? How do I relate to my family, and how do I relate to my Christian brothers and sisters in this? 1 Corinthians 8-10 spoke powerfully to their situation.

However, it did more than that. As I kept preaching and working away at Paul's approach to these matters, the whole doctrine of Christian liberty tumbled out, which is so essential to maintaining justification by faith alone. And as that became clearer, it revolutionized my approach to personal counselling. The fashion of the time was 'indirect counselling', in which the counsellor never said anything to anyone about anything apart from, "Mmm, really? Yes, I see what you mean. Mmm. Yes." It was a very attractive method. Even I could do it because you never actually had to say to anyone, "I think you should …" or "I think that's foolish" or "I think that's wise", let alone "I think that's right" or "I think that's wrong".

But with a thorough doctrine of Christian liberty, you are free to say to people, "Well, I think you should do X in these circumstances, but if you do the opposite, I'll support you thoroughly because it's a matter of freedom. If you want my ideas, I think this is the wisest way to go. But it's your choice, not mine, and I'll back you either way." This is very important, because it also allows you to say, "No, that is wrong" on some occasions, without being heard to say that on every occasion when you offer advice.

This all came out of 1 Corinthians 8-10 and food offered to idols, a subject I would never have thought of preaching on in a million years. 1 Corinthians 8-10 also began to show me *the difference between strategy and tactics* in evangelism (and in ministry generally), and it is this topic I want to particularly address here. The key section is 1 Corinthians 10:31-11:1:

> So, whether you eat or drink, or whatever you do, do all to the glory of God. Give no offense to Jews or to Greeks or to the church of God, just as I try to please everyone in everything I do, not seeking my own advantage, but that of many, that they may be saved.
>
> Be imitators of me, as I am of Christ.

I think it is this passage, more than any other in the New Testament, that places a great imperative upon us (i.e. every Christian) to evangelize. If we are to grow like Christ, and be imitators of Christ like the apostle Paul, then we should try to please everyone in everything we do in order that they may be saved.

The Lord Jesus Christ lived (and died) to the glory of his Father, and we should do whatever we do to the glory of God—especially and including evangelism. The chief end and purpose of evangelism is the chief end and purpose of all humans: to glorify God and enjoy him forever. We don't evangelize to save souls but to glorify God. That's the primary thing; the saving of souls is secondary.

This is one of those important Arminian/Calvinist distinctions. If I forget that glorifying God is primary, and have as my primary aim the saving of souls, my temptation will be to do anything I can, and change whatever needs changing, in order to save more souls. Furthermore, if I succeed, I will puff myself up, and if I fail, I will depress myself.

But if the aim is to glorify God by preaching his gospel, I know that it will be a sweet smell of salvation for some, but a stench of death in the nostrils of others. And I don't have to take responsibility for that decision, or that effect; I place the gospel in front of people, and it is God's Spirit who brings them salvation or the hardening of their hearts. My aim is only ever this: to glorify God in my speaking of the gospel. This means that faithfulness is the test of true evangelism, not success (as Paul makes very clear earlier in 1 Corinthians 4).

But notice what glorifying God in faithful evangelism also involves here in 1 Corinthians 10: it means offering no unnecessary offence. We don't want to put anything in anyone's way except the gospel. And so Paul, who so adamantly insists in other places that he is *not* a man-pleaser, here is proud to be a man-pleaser—not for his own benefit or to make his life easier or to have more friends, but for their salvation. He will change his eating and drinking habits freely in order to glorify God by presenting the gospel to them.

So the Lord seems to be saying two things to us through the apostle Paul:

1. We must glorify God by faithfully and invariably sticking to the task God has given us: to preach the unchanging gospel of Christ.
2. We must be prepared to be flexible and to use our Christian liberty to change our approach from moment to moment, and person to person, as the circumstances require.

In modern terms, Paul is talking about the difference between strategy and tactics. I'm sure, like me, you have endured strategic planning sessions where nearly the entire time is consumed in a debate over the differences between words like 'mission' and 'vision' and 'purpose' and 'strategy' and 'tactics'! I am using the words as the *Macquarie Dictionary* defines them:

> **strategy:** noun. generalship; the science or art of combining and employing the means of war in planning and directing large military movements and operations.
>
> **tactics:** plural noun. the art or science of disposing military or naval forces for battle and manoeuvring them in battle.[13]

Strategy is the big thinking—the overall plan and the means for getting there. Strategy is done by prime ministers and generals who say, "If we're going to win World War II, we'll have to land

---

13. *The Macquarie Dictionary Online* © 2008 Macquarie Dictionary Publishers Pty Ltd.

an invasion force in France, backed up by air support". Tactics is more immediate thinking: it's manoeuvring the pieces on the chessboard to achieve the smaller milestones that go together to make up the strategy. Tactics is done by colonels and captains who say, "We'll need to land this many troops at this time and in this place, depending on the tides and the weather, in order to secure a beachhead, with this many planes running these missions in support".

If the strategy is to win the war by invading France, then there may be a number of legitimate tactical approaches to getting that done. But these options wouldn't include sending flowers, or running up the white flag, or deciding to land an invasion force in Greenland instead. Tactics sit under strategy, and are circumscribed by strategy.

In Christian ministry, as in war and business, we must have a clear understanding of not only what our strategy is, but also how it relates to the day-to-day tactics. This is particularly important for Christians, because our strategy is not something we have to come up with at a vision-planning day. Our strategy is understood by revelation. It is *God's* strategy—his cosmic plan—and his way of getting it done.

Let's look first at God's strategy, and how it involves us, before returning to the question of tactics.

The strategy of God

We can describe the strategy of God in trinitarian fashion by starting with the big plan of God the Father, as Paul expresses it in Ephesians 1. These are well-known words, but look at them again closely. What is the Father's goal and how does he plan to achieve it?

> Blessed be the God and Father of our Lord Jesus Christ,
> who has blessed us in Christ with every spiritual blessing

> in the heavenly places, even as he chose us in him before the foundation of the world, that we should be holy and blameless before him. In love he predestined us for adoption as sons through Jesus Christ, according to the purpose of his will, to the praise of his glorious grace, with which he has blessed us in the Beloved. In him we have redemption through his blood, the forgiveness of our trespasses, according to the riches of his grace, which he lavished upon us, in all wisdom and insight making known to us the mystery of his will, according to his purpose, which he set forth in Christ as a plan for the fullness of time, to unite all things in him, things in heaven and things on earth.
>
> In him we have obtained an inheritance, having been predestined according to the purpose of him who works all things according to the counsel of his will, so that we who were the first to hope in Christ might be to the praise of his glory. In him you also, when you heard the word of truth, the gospel of your salvation, and believed in him, were sealed with the promised Holy Spirit, who is the guarantee of our inheritance until we acquire possession of it, to the praise of his glory. (Eph 1:3-14)

We might summarize Paul's summary like this: God's ultimate goal is to unite all things under Christ, and he is sovereignly working to achieve this by sealing people (both Jews *and* Gentiles) with the Holy Spirit as they hear the word of truth, the gospel of Christ. The plan of God, right from the very beginning, was to include both Jews and Gentiles in one people, and central to this plan was the redemption that was won through Christ's blood, and the preaching of that gospel to all the nations.

Jesus says much the same thing in Luke 24 after his death and resurrection. He tells his gobsmacked disciples that everything written about him in the Law and the Prophets *must* be fulfilled, and then he elaborates: "Thus it is written, that the Christ should suffer and on the third day rise from the dead, and that repentance and forgiveness of sins should be proclaimed in his name to all nations, beginning from Jerusalem" (Luke 24:46-47). This is the strategy of God for gathering his elect people from all over the world: that the Christ should suffer and rise, and that the gospel of repentance and forgiveness should be preached to all nations.

It is not just the Father's strategy, it is also the work of Christ himself: "I will build my church", says Jesus in Matthew 16:18. Christ's work is the gathering together of his own people into his own assembly—his church. He is the builder of the congregation, and you and I are only subcontractors. He may choose to use you and me in his building work, but it is *his* work and *his* activity. 1 Corinthians 3 expresses this delightfully:

> What then is Apollos? What is Paul? Servants through whom you believed, as the Lord assigned to each. I planted, Apollos watered, but God gave the growth. So neither he who plants nor he who waters is anything, but only God who gives the growth. He who plants and he who waters are one, and each will receive his wages according to his labor. For we are God's fellow workers. You are God's field, God's building. (1 Cor 3:5-9)

We have a job to do, and we must do it faithfully—whether it be planting or watering, and so on. But it is God's job to grow the congregation, not your job or my job. It is *his* growth, not our growth, because Christ is building his assembly. He is the builder; we are the fellow workers—a title and role of high honour that also makes it very clear who is the builder and who is not.

Christ is building his congregation according to the eternal plan of the Father by the preaching of the gospel to all the nations. Who does this preaching? 1 Peter 1 has a surprising answer for us:

> Concerning this salvation, the prophets who prophesied about the grace that was to be yours searched and inquired carefully, inquiring what person or time the Spirit of Christ in them was indicating when he predicted the sufferings of Christ and the subsequent glories. It was revealed to them that they were serving not themselves but you, in the things that have now been announced to you through those who preached the good news to you by the Holy Spirit sent from heaven, things into which angels long to look. (1 Pet 1:10-12)

This passage contains a sentence of such length and complexity to rival Paul's in Ephesians 1! But look closely. Who is the evangelist?

It is the Holy Spirit. The Holy Spirit has been sent from heaven to proclaim the fulfillment of those things that he had previously indicated through the prophets—that is, the sufferings of Christ and the subsequent glories. These are realities into which angels long to look. But you have it all over the angels, says Peter, because these things have now been announced to you through those who preached the gospel *by the Holy Spirit sent from heaven*.

It's a complicated little passage, but its logic is thoroughly in line with what we have already seen about the strategy of God: Christ is building his church, and he is doing it through us. The Holy Spirit is preaching the gospel, and he is doing it through us. And this is all according to the eternal plan of the Father to sum up all things in Christ Jesus, to the praise of his glory.

Our part in God's strategy

God has a strategy, a big plan of action that is heading towards a goal. But as we have already begun to see, his strategy involves our actions. It is *his* work and *his* strategy, but in his incredible grace, he puts it into effect through us.

What are the actions God gives us to do as part of his strategy? Here are the three absolutely essential ones:

1. Prayer

When Paul first preached the gospel to the Thessalonians, he knew that they were among Christ's chosen people because "our gospel came to you not only in word, but also in power and in the Holy Spirit and with full conviction" (1 Thess 1:5). Their wholehearted, Spirit-empowered response showed them to be among those that Christ was building into his congregation.

In other words, the Holy Spirit was not only the evangelist (speaking through Paul); he was also at work in the hearers—in the Thessalonians—so that they were completely convinced about the truth of the message. Later Paul says that they embraced his gospel "not as the word of men but as what it really is, the word of God" (1 Thess 2:13). And when he writes to them again, Paul urges them to pray for him—that "the word of the Lord may speed ahead and be honored, as happened among you" (2 Thess 3:1).

It is precisely because the growth of the gospel is God's work by his Spirit (both in the preaching and in the response that people make) that our first and primary action is prayer. We need to keep asking God to glorify himself by preaching his message by the Holy Spirit throughout the world. We need to beg him to send the gospel out, and through its preaching, to save people and build Christ's congregation. And we pray this because we know it is his plan.

Christians are not fatalists. We know what God's will and plan is—that his kingdom would come, that his will would be done on earth, that his name would be hallowed—but we don't just sit back and say, "Well, it's going to happen anyway, so ... whatever". No, we pray (as our Lord taught us) that God would fulfill his plan for the world, and soon. We pray, "Please, Lord, bring it on!"

I love the way Paul also asks for prayer from the Ephesians. He asks them to pray for him "that words may be given to me in opening my mouth boldly to proclaim the mystery of the gospel, for which I am an ambassador in chains, that I may declare it boldly, as I ought to speak" (Eph 6:19-20). Most of us who have been Christians for a long time are used to thinking of Paul as one of the valiant men of the faith—a fearless champion of the gospel, ready to speak up for Christ in all circumstances. But you don't pray for what you already have, so it must have been the case that Paul lacked boldness, like the rest of us. Other people always look bold when they're speaking about Christ (whether in public or in conversation), but it's rarely like that behind their eyeballs; they are usually just as terrified as we are.

Prayer, then, is the first and primary task God has graciously given to us as his fellow workers. He uses our prayers in his purposes, and so we must pray—really pray. Set aside time to pray. Drop something else so you can pray—like the apostles had to in Acts 6, where they said:

> "It is not right that we should give up preaching the word of God to serve tables. Therefore, brothers, pick out from among you seven men of good repute, full of the Spirit and of wisdom, whom we will appoint to this duty. But we will devote ourselves to prayer and to the ministry of the word." (Acts 6:2b-4)

2. Proclamation

This brings us to the second necessity: proclamation. I will not dwell long on the central and crucial place of proclamation—or preaching or announcing or telling or speaking or whatever similar verb you wish to use. Of the many, many New Testament passages we could look at to establish the vital place proclaiming God's word has in God's strategy, it's hard to go past the simple truth of Romans 10:17: "faith comes from hearing, and hearing through the word of Christ". The strategy of God is for his Spirit to preach the Word through us, and so to elicit faith from those who hear.

We could look at Paul's solemn charge to Timothy: "preach the word; be ready in season and out of season" (2 Tim 4:2), or his marvellous little summary of his ministry in 2 Corinthians 4, which consists of the plain open statement of the truth of the gospel that Jesus Christ is Lord. I rather suspect that the central place of proclamation in the strategy of God is not something most of us need convincing about—at least theoretically. However, like Timothy, we may need a solemn and scary charge to get on with it—especially given how easy it is to give up on proclamation, to be distracted from it, to be discouraged by how plain and unexciting it seems, to be tempted to try some other method, and so on.

I well remember a highly intelligent young man who came to see me on campus years ago. He had read BF Skinner and other atheists, and had himself become a convinced, thoroughgoing atheist. As a result, he was suicidal. He was intelligent enough to see that consistent atheism drained life of any meaning, purpose or joy. His existence was just an accident, as was everything else. He had tried all the joys that Solomon tried in Ecclesiastes, and had come to the same conclusion: it was all absurd and pointless. He wanted some way out of the prison of despair that he found himself in, but didn't know how to find it.

I proceeded to discuss the philosophy of atheism with him over several weeks. I presented a great many clever arguments (well, at least I thought they were clever), but got absolutely nowhere. Then my good friend and colleague Col Marshall said to the young man, "Look, faith comes from hearing the word of God. So why don't you just come along to church and listen for a while?"

You can guess what happened. That young man came along to church and listened, and was converted. It had nothing to do with clever apologetics because, in the end, you can't argue someone into the kingdom. Faith comes from hearing the word of God.

That's our task in the strategy of God: to keep proclaiming the word of God so that the Holy Spirit, who preaches it through us and who also works in the hearts of the hearers, will bring people to faith.

3. People

The third task that God has given us is implicit in the first two, but needs to be stated on its own: the third part of our work is people. When Jesus looks out upon the crowds, he is filled with compassion because they are like sheep without a shepherd (Matt 9:36). It's the same compassion that God has for the world—a compassion that causes him to send his only Son for its salvation (John 3:16). But what is the 'world' that God loves? It is people opposed to God.

We saw this in our look at 1 Corinthians 8-10 earlier in this article. "I put myself out for *other people*", says Paul. "I will gladly inconvenience myself, and put aside my own likes and dislikes, because I want to win *people*."

The work God has given us to do is focused on and directed towards people, not institutions or organizations or programs. All our structures and programs must serve *people*. This is so obvious, it seems facile to repeat it. But judging by what we see in Christian ministry, it needs to be repeated. We get this back to front all the time, and end up with institutions and programs and structures that seem to exist for their own sake. In fact, it often feels like the people are there to serve *them* (i.e. the programs), not vice versa.

We must never lose sight of *people* and their place in God's strategy. His work is directed *towards* people, and it takes place *through* people—which is why the risen Christ commissions his disciples to make other disciples in Matthew 28. Every Christian is to be a disciple-making disciple. I won't say more on this point—my friends Col Marshall and Tony Payne have written at length about it in their excellent book, *The Trellis and the Vine*.

The tactics of man

God's strategy—including our part in it—is a given. It's not up to us to figure out what Christian ministry is really about; the big plan and the strategy for getting there is revealed to us by God, and as with all revelation, our response must be to believe it and act upon it.

The strategy for our action is set for us: we need to be praying, we need to be proclaiming and we need to be focusing on people. These three key strategies should determine the activity of every church and Christian ministry. When we meet to think about how we are going, and to plan what we will do next, our discussion should not centre on devising a strategy, it should centre on considering how well and faithfully we are implementing God's strategy.

Remember, strategy is the higher-level thinking: it's laying down the key directions and activities we are going to undertake to achieve the objective. And it is given by God. Tactics are short-term, immediate actions to do with how the strategy will play out in the next five minutes, the next five days or the next five months.

Tactical thinking is important and valuable, but secondary. Tactics sit under strategy, and support strategy. In fact, one of the big problems in any business enterprise is making sure that the day-to-day actions and activities of the business actually relate to the strategy—or are 'aligned', as the jargon goes. What often happens in the real world is that tactical decisions tend to take on a life of their own, and end up hiving off in a different direction to the strategy, or even undermining the strategy. Or sometimes we end up with 'orphan' activities that once had some connection with the company strategy, but which have long since ceased to make any contribution to it.

It hardly needs to be said that this happens in churches all the time. A particular ministry is set up—let's say a kids' club—as a tactic to proclaim the gospel to the kids of the suburb prayerfully. It all goes well, and makes a useful contribution to the overall prayer-proclamation-people strategy for some years. But in time, the suburb changes. Young families are squeezed out by higher real estate prices. The demographic profile changes, and the tactical usefulness of this particular way of proclaiming the gospel evaporates. But any suggestion that perhaps we should shut down the kids' club will usually be met with vigorous protest—not from the kids (there aren't any), but from people in the church who have been working in and supporting this ministry for years.

Tactics are provisional and change constantly. They can vary from moment to moment. I meet a Jew, and so I become a Jew to reach this Jew. The strategy hasn't changed; I will need to be praying for him, and proclaiming to him, and loving him as a person, but my particular approach and behaviour will change because he is a Jew. And likewise, when I meet a Gentile five minutes later, the immediate tactics will change. In a big multicultural city like Sydney (where I live), I can experience minute-by-minute tactical variations as I meet Chinese people, Africans, Indians, old-fashioned Anglo-Saxons, Roman Catholics, Buddhists, atheists, agnostics, young people, old people, and so on.

Tactics are secondary, provisional, and almost always break down and fail eventually. Even a superb bit of tactical thinking about how to reach out to a particular group will almost certainly be rendered inappropriate or unsuccessful over time.

Our problem is that we think too highly of our tactics, and even confuse them with the strategy. We think that if only we come up with the right tactical moves, then success will be ours, and God's kingdom will explode everywhere. And if we do achieve some success, we are only all the more emboldened to think that we have 'cracked it', and so we write a book and become a church growth expert.

Most 'church growth' literature is really short-term, localized tactical thinking, but it often masquerades as something far more grand. It often oversells itself as 'strategy', and as the new secret to ministry success.

Understanding the difference between God's strategy and our tactics is also important in liberating us to try different things, and to let other people try different things (back to Christian liberty again). For example, some churches seek to proclaim the gospel prayerfully to the people in their community by putting on really attractive well-run church meetings, and drawing in outsiders to hear the Word. These 'attractional' churches often have excellent kids' programs, good car parks, polished music, effective marketing and highly gifted preachers. Given that they are driven by God's strategy and they really do give their time to prayer, proclamation and people, these sorts of churches can do wonderful work under God's strategy and see many people saved. They are an excellent example of a group that is willing to put themselves out and do whatever they can, tactically speaking, to seek the salvation of people, as Christ did.

However, other churches take a different tactical approach. For example, some operate in small, highly committed teams, living in closer Christian community and proclaiming the gospel prayerfully through small group meetings, household gatherings, and personal community contacts and networks. Yet other groups might try a blend of these tactical approaches, or some other approach altogether.

Our problem comes when we absolutize our tactics, and raise them to the level of strategy—as if all ministries and churches must adopt the same tactics to be 'successful' or, indeed, to be faithful. We must remember: God is the one with the plan and the strategy, and he is putting his strategy into effect through us. The success and the results are not up to us, because it is only as God gives the growth through his Holy Spirit that God achieves his own purposes. We are subcontractors, agents, fellow workers. It's not up to us to figure it all out and make it work; our job is faithful adherence to the strategy of God.

First published in *The Briefing*, no. 358/9, July/August 2008 (thebriefing.com.au).

Appendix II

Preach the negative as well as the positive

I had just met one of the wiser older saints of North American Christianity. We were walking together to an evening dinner party. Apropos of nothing, he said to me, "Phillip, when men grow old, some of them go soft-headed and sentimental, while others become cantankerous and irascible". It was a strange lesson to be given, but I understood what he meant about an hour later when he seated me between two elderly preachers. In these two men, I discovered a classic illustration of each type. I had been warned!

Over the next few days, I listened to both these men preach, and, sure enough, one was negative and the other positive. I saw, in those few days, a very common pattern of two different styles of preaching: an affirmative style that looks in the text for positive things to say about people, and a negative style that always finds in the text things to criticize about others or the congregation.

Some people preach with great fervour sermons that are little more than reflections of their personality, emphasizing the positive or the negative in the text and in the congregation. These sermons have less to do with 'speaking the words of God' than reflecting the personality of the preacher. Either he will place his personality upon the text, or he will select only those texts that reflect his personality. However, faithful explication of the text in an ordered fashion will sometimes be negative and sometimes be positive, for both are found in the Bible irrespective of the preacher's personality.

Reasons for affirmative preaching

Leaving personality aside, the current choice for most preachers today is the affirmative over the negative. There are several reasons for this choice. First, society at large pushes the preacher in this direction. Educational models promote the effectiveness of the affirmative style of teaching, as do most studies in advertising and public relations. Also, the relativism of today's postmodern thought is positive about all statements—all statements, that is, except negations! The ideology of a multicultural society requires positivity about alternative views, and frowns upon any communication that threatens the fragile peace that has been established between communities.

Second, the current climate in religious circles favours affirmative preaching. Courses in pastoral counselling point to the advantages of non-judgemental, positive communication. Pastors have to perform. The key to evaluation is no longer God's judgement on the last day (1 Cor 4:1-5), but growth in congregational numbers, budget and buildings. Leaders in the church are tempted to be like modern politicians, leading by following the popular sentiments expressed in surveys and polls.

Third, the pastor's own congregation often pushes him to preach affirmatively. These churches do not choose ministers to change them, but rather those who will confirm them in their current beliefs and practices. There is a feedback system at work. The affirmative preacher is affirmed by the congregation into greater affirmation in his preaching, while the negative preacher is constantly negated out of preaching negatively. There are hardly any attempts these days to negate affirmative preaching or to affirm negative preaching. Our sinful desire to be well-thought-of by people encourages us to think well of them and to speak positively to them. The pressure on pastors to maintain what is already there—and therefore to preach positive sermons that unite all parties in the congregation—is massive. The sinful hearts of the preacher and the congregation seek pleasant, peaceful things that will confirm them in their sinfulness, rather than remind them of judgement and challenge them to repent.

Advantages of affirmative preaching

Even though we face these pressures, there are advantages to affirmative preaching. The affirmative preacher rightly reflects the generous graciousness of our God and Saviour, and the gospel we preach. It does not befit the gospel of grace to see a mean-spirited negative preacher denouncing everything and everybody.

Evangelistically, the affirmative preacher, being more inclusive in his language, content and manner, will be appreciated by a larger and wider audience. His width of appeal makes it easier for the congregation to invite all sorts and conditions of men to hear the message. When people come, they are less likely to be offended by trivial, minor and irrelevant issues as the preacher will be more attuned to confirm them in their present position.

Pastorally, the more affirmative preacher will establish and develop relationships within the congregation that will enable him to minister privately to people. Non-confrontational, non-judgemental attitudes from the pulpit increase people's openness to talk about problems, issues and sinfulness, knowing that the preacher is sympathetic and supportive.

Disadvantages of affirmative preaching

Over time, however, people come to understand that a preacher who is always positive cannot be trusted with the truth. He may make you feel good, but he is not addressing the real issues of life. The public relations kind of saccharine preacher is first loved, believed and trusted, then questioned, doubted and, finally, despised.

The positive preacher finds it very difficult to change roles in private counselling to say anything negative. People who come to him will not expect to hear the truth, but to be confirmed in their opinions. Being negative about a topic when speaking to a congregation is considerably easier than being negative to a person about his behaviour privately and face-to-face.

Affirmative preaching encourages ministers to be 'men pleasers' (Gal 1:10). I cannot recall speaking publicly against Roman Catholicism without being criticized, even though, as a Protestant, I should be expected to be critical of Roman Catholicism. Yet whenever I make even a small positive mention of Rome, I am always commended by people.

Woe unto you, said Jesus, when all speak well of you, and blessed are you when men revile you and say all manner of falsehood against you because of me. Rejoice and be glad for this is how they treated the prophets of old and because your reward in the kingdom of heaven will be great (cf. Matt 5:11-12). These words are not necessary for those who are called to preach a popular message, but for those whose task is likely to lead to unpopularity.

Biblical evaluation

The outcome of an action should not be ignored, but Christians ought to make decisions based on the rightness of the action, not its outcome. The rightness of an action is revealed in the Scriptures.

Because God is the author of Scripture and the creator of the world, we can expect the right actions, revealed in Scripture, to have the best outcome in God's world. Sometimes these outcomes will be long-term rather than immediate. Sometimes it is only in eternity that we will be able to see the outcomes or the value of the outcomes.

In preaching, we are instructed by God to speak the very words of God (1 Pet 4:11). These words from God are sometimes negative and sometimes positive. The faithful preacher will deliver both as they arise. As it is the negative that currently needs reinstating in our culture, let us look at that side of the Bible's teaching.

First, we must note the biblical evidence for negative preaching. It was the false prophets in Jeremiah's day who preached "Peace, peace" when there was no peace (Jer 6:14, 8:11). Isaiah's task in preaching was to confirm people in the judgement that was coming upon them. Nathan was not affirming King David when he said, "You are the man!" (2 Sam 12:7). It was Paul who had to contend with Peter—and even Barnabas—over the truth of the gospel by opposing Peter to his face (Gal 2:11-13). It was our Lord Jesus himself who preached woes, who warned people of the coming division that he was bringing, and who called upon people to hate even their closest family members (Matt 10:34-37). Remember, Jesus was the one who introduced the word 'gehenna' (i.e. 'hell').

Second, we need to note that certain key concepts are, by their very nature, negative. The classic example is repentance, since it means the denunciation and renunciation of our present and former lives. It is to say "No" to yourself, as well as taking up the cross and following Jesus. Paul described his settled evangelistic ministry in terms of "testifying both to Jews and to Greeks of repentance toward God and of faith in our Lord Jesus Christ" (Acts 20:21).

Just as becoming a Christian requires this negative action of repentance, so growing and going on as a Christian requires negating ourselves. Being led by the Spirit of God requires all Christians to "put to death the deeds of the body" (Rom 8:13), as our dying with Christ also requires us to "Put to death therefore what is earthly in you" (Col 3:5). Mortification is negative, painful work, but one that will bring forth great joy.

Third, the preacher must preach in such a way as to negate the sinful, worldly and self-determining patterns of fallen humanity. Not in the way of the world, but by divine power he must fight, demolish strongholds, and take every thought captive to Christ by destroying arguments and every pretension that sets itself up against the knowledge of God (cf. 2 Cor 10:4-5). The preacher must not just flee idolatry personally; he must also denounce it and warn others against it. The prophets of old used sarcastic mockery to ridicule idolatry. The overseer is not only to exhort in sound doctrine; he is also to refute those who contradict it (Titus 1:9).

The preacher is called upon to use the word of God in the way it was intended, which includes negative preaching. Since God's word teaches, rebukes, corrects and trains in righteousness (2 Tim 3:16), so the preacher must teach, correct, rebuke and train in righteousness with great patience and care.

Fourth, the logical power of the negative is found in the text of Scripture itself. The more powerful part of Jesus' words is not his claim that he is the way, the truth and the life, but that there is no other way to the Father except through him (John 14:6). Similarly, to say that somebody should be born again is not as strong as to say that no-one can see the kingdom of God unless he is born again (John 3:3).

Advantages of preaching negatively

The power and clarifying effect of the negative is why preachers today must also preach negatively. For some years, we have run university missions under the title 'Know Christ, Know Life'. It is a useful pun, for we are also able to preach on 'No Christ, No Life'.

Most people patiently patronize the positive expression ('Know Christ, Know Life'). They feel glad that knowing Christ has been such a positive experience for us that we now feel in touch with life itself. They have had the same experience through Buddha or transcendentalism or even golf. However, when we preach the negative, they become angry because we are confronting them with the claims of Christ. The negative proclaims more clearly that, without Christ, there is no life. Thus we make clear what we mean when we say that, with Christ, we know life.

In an age of postmodern relativism, any assertion is believed, but the hardest ones to accept are negatives. When all views are equally valid, negative views push the relativism into the absurd—from which some people recoil.

But it is not just evangelistic preaching that needs to be negative. Christians need to be warned about the dire consequences of continuing in sin. Some evangelicals believe in sin theoretically, but are too naive and trusting of human nature in practice.

In today's cultural climate, it is important that preachers—in particular, pastors—have the courage to address issues as they appear in the Scriptures. For example, we must not avoid potentially divisive passages like 1 Timothy 2 (and what it says about men and women and authority) for the sake of holding the congregation together and causing no offence. It is critical that preachers negate the feminist world view as it collides with biblical truth. This must be done both in terms of the world outside the church, and in terms of the inroads that feminism has made among Christian people. To preach only those aspects of the relationship between men and women where the world and the Bible agree is to distort not only the Bible as a whole, but also the very passages where there is agreement—because they come in the context of a Bible that is quite alien to feminism.

Avoiding the negative in order to maintain unity creates a false unity. The unity is preserved by the personality or charisma of the minister, and by the fact that the divisive issues are never addressed. All seems well on the face of it but, underneath, deep divisions exist. When the minister leaves, the tensions come boiling to the surface, the differing viewpoints enter into conflict, and the new minister inherits a war zone. Indeed, the selection panel for the new minister may find itself divided, or suddenly not sure what the fundamental theological stance of the congregation really is. This can lead to a new minister being selected who takes the congregation off in a completely different direction theologically. It all stems from a failure of the preacher to preach the whole truth of the Scriptures, including the negative.

It is really at the point of negating that we discover whether we have confidence in God's word. Martin Luther put it with typical power:

> If I profess with the loudest voice and clearest exposition every portion of the truth of God except precisely that little point which the world and the devil are at the moment attacking, I am not confessing Christ, however boldly I may be professing Christ. Where the battle rages, there the loyalty of the soldier is proved, and to be steady on all the battle front besides, is mere flight and disgrace if he flinches at that point.[14]

---

14. Martin Luther, *Luther's Works*, Weimar edition, Briefewchsel [Correspondence], vol. 3, tr. Dr Werner Gitt, Concordia, St Louis, p. 81, cited in GA Lindbeck, *The Nature of Doctrine: Religion and Theology in a Postliberal Age*, Westminster John Knox Press, Louisville, 1984, p. 75.

Negative preaching is not everything, and it is not to be encouraged as an expression of personality, but it does need a good deal of affirmation in order that it might return to its rightful place among those who would speak the very words of God.

First published in *The Journal for Biblical Manhood and Womanhood*, vol. 5, no. 2, Fall 2000 (cbmw.org). Adapted and reproduced with permission.

Appendix III

Tips for young preachers

Experienced preachers often get asked by young preachers to give them advice on their craft. How do I preach better? Should I preach longer? Or shorter? Should I use illustrations? Should I use a full script or just notes? Each preacher develops opinions on these things, and before long the young preacher is offering advice to the even-younger preacher.

There are certainly techniques and approaches to preaching that can be learned. There is also an element to it that seems to spring more naturally from the personality. A combination of learning techniques and listening to your mentors will most likely help you to achieve the goal of faithful, thorough and motivating Bible preaching.

Below is a list of tips for those who are beginning to preach. They are not an exhaustive program for preaching effectively; rather, they are simple ideas that seem to bring more success than failure.

1. When you preach, be as good as you can

This seems like stating the obvious, but it is a good thing to keep in the forefront of your mind as you begin a preaching life. Preaching is the central reason that the church gathers; it is the speaking of God's very word, for the salvation of souls and the building of the church. Preaching is always worth the extra effort.

What's more, if your congregation is used to biblical, expository preaching, they may tolerate you being a little boring now and then, because their faith in the Bible lets them know it's still worth listening. This is no excuse to slacken off, and work half-heartedly on your sermons! However, if you are trying to persuade a congregation that is used to another form of preaching that expositional preaching is especially valuable, your sermon and delivery must be especially good.

2. Fledgling preachers tend to be boring

If you're not boring when you emerge from theological college, you probably didn't learn anything. Your head will be full of theology, Greek phrases, the latest ideas on running a church, and whatever else has grabbed your intellectual fancy.

Five years out of college, if you're still boring, you have a problem.

However, it is better to come out of college and preach heavy sermons than to come out of college and be too light. If that is the case, in five years time you may have nothing left to say.

3. Work out how long you can preach for and still be interesting

To do this, you need people you trust in the congregation who can give you good feedback—who can tell you that by 35 minutes no-one was listening any more! If you learn you're a 35-minute preacher, then make sure you do the job in those 35 minutes. Don't feel you have to preach for 45 minutes just because someone else does. Having said that, if someone tells you after your first sermon that you should keep it to ten minutes from here on in, that shouldn't dictate your sermon length for the rest of your life. Give yourself a chance.

4. Know how to use commentaries

Commentaries can be useful tools, but they can be deadening for preachers. Spend more time in the biblical text and thinking for yourself about it, and less time answering the problems of the commentators. Scholars who write commentaries are usually talking to each other, answering each others' questions. They are not the questions that the person in the pew has, and they're often not what the text is about either. Even the best biblical commentators still have to answer many questions entirely irrelevant to the people you are serving on a Sunday morning. Knowing the answers to these questions is still important, but you can't let it take up all your sermon preparation time, let alone your congregation's valuable time as they listen to you preach.

5. Find the logic units of the book; don't just preach on chapters or paragraphs

The Bible must determine the sermon. A book like Proverbs, for instance, is not suited to chapter-by-chapter exposition. On the other hand, you might want to take John 3:16 on its own. It is crucial to understand the logic of the material you are preaching.

6. Young preachers should start with bigger sections

Preaching on large slabs of Scripture means you are less likely to read your own agenda into the text. Preaching on one or two verses takes much more knowledge in order to get it right. With longer passages, the congregation will be able to hear the

Bible speaking for itself. As you grow and learn more, you can more easily and legitimately preach full sermons on shorter passages without eisegesis.

7. Expository preaching is worth fighting for (but a lot of other things are not)

If expository preaching is a new concept for your congregation, go easy on everything else. It is important that you establish the priority of teaching the Bible. It's also important that you love your congregation and that they learn to love you. Live your life with them, care for them in all the ways they appreciate, and don't change things you don't have to. If they know you love them, they will be much more willing to accept your leadership in preaching the Bible.

First published in *The Briefing*, no. 279, December 2001 (thebriefing.com.au).

matthiasmedia

Matthias Media is an evangelical publishing ministry that seeks to persuade all Christians of the truth of God's purposes in Jesus Christ as revealed in the Bible, and equip them with high-quality resources, so that by the work of the Holy Spirit they will:

- abandon their lives to the honour and service of Christ in daily holiness and decision-making
- pray constantly in Christ's name for the fruitfulness and growth of his gospel
- speak the Bible's life-changing word whenever and however they can— in the home, in the world and in the fellowship of his people.

Our wide range of resources includes Bible studies, books, training courses, tracts and children's material. To find out more, and to access samples and free downloads, visit our website:

matthiasmedia.com

How to buy our resources

1. Direct from us over the internet:
   - in the US: matthiasmedia.com
   - in Australia: matthiasmedia.com.au

2. Direct from us by phone: please visit our website for current phone contact information.

3. Through a range of outlets in various parts of the world. Visit **matthiasmedia.com/contact** for details about recommended retailers in your part of the world.

4. Trade enquiries can be addressed to:
   - in the US and Canada: sales@matthiasmedia.com
   - in Australia and the rest of the world: sales@matthiasmedia.com.au

For more resources by Phillip Jensen, visit **phillipjensen.com**.

Register at our website for our **free** regular email update to receive information about the latest new resources, **exclusive special offers**, and free articles to help you grow in your Christian life and ministry.

Also from Matthias Media

The Trellis and the Vine

All Christian ministry is a mixture of trellis and vine.

There is vine work: the prayerful preaching and teaching of the word of God to see people converted and grow to maturity as disciples of Christ. And there is trellis work: creating and maintaining the physical and organizational structures and programs that support vine work and its growth.

What's the state of the trellis and the vine in your part of the world? Has trellis work taken over, as it has a habit of doing? Is the vine work being done by very few (perhaps only the pastor and only on Sundays)? And is the vine starting to wilt as a result?

In *The Trellis and the Vine*, Colin Marshall and Tony Payne answer afresh urgent fundamental questions about Christian ministry. They dig back into the Bible's view of Christian ministry, and argue that a major mind-shift is required if we are to fulfill the Great Commission of Christ, and see the vine flourish again.

> *"This is the best book I've read on the nature of church ministry."*
>
> Mark Dever, Senior Pastor, Capitol Hill Baptist Church

FOR MORE INFORMATION OR TO ORDER CONTACT:

Matthias Media
sales@matthiasmedia.com.au
matthiasmedia.com.au

Matthias Media (USA)
sales@matthiasmedia.com
matthiasmedia.com

Also from Matthias Media

Setting Hearts on Fire
A guide to giving evangelistic talks

"Were not our hearts burning within us while he talked with us on the road and opened the Scriptures to us?" (Luke 24:32)

Anyone who explains the good news of Jesus Christ to others hopes that this will be the result—that hearts will be set on fire by the message, and that repentance and faith will follow.

In this book, which is the fruit of his 40 years experience as an evangelist, John Chapman passes on the skills of his craft. He explains how telling people the gospel of Jesus Christ requires us to be servants: servants of the word itself (to understand it accurately), and servants of the people (to explain it clearly).

Whether you are a person who teaches the Bible in a Sunday School class, a small group Bible study, Scripture at school, a teenage fellowship group or through preaching sermons, then this book is for you. In his inimitable way, 'Chappo' shows you, step by step, how to prepare and deliver a talk that clearly communicates the gospel of Jesus Christ.

FOR MORE INFORMATION OR TO ORDER CONTACT:

Matthias Media
sales@matthiasmedia.com.au
matthiasmedia.com.au

Matthias Media (USA)
sales@matthiasmedia.com
matthiasmedia.com

Also by Paul Grimmond

Right Side Up

"I set out to write a book for new Christians, to explain what it means to be a Christian and what the lifelong adventure of following Jesus is like. But I soon realized that what Jesus wants to say to a new Christian is really the same thing he wants to keep saying to the seasoned saint: "Whoever loses his life for my sake will find it". My prayer is that this book will persuade you of the truth of those words, and help you live like you believe them. It's a book for the brand new Christian that should challenge every believer—whether you've been following Jesus for five minutes or 50 years."

Author, Paul Grimmond

FOR MORE INFORMATION OR TO ORDER CONTACT:

Matthias Media
sales@matthiasmedia.com.au
matthiasmedia.com.au

Matthias Media (USA)
sales@matthiasmedia.com
matthiasmedia.com

By Phillip Jensen

Guidance and the Voice of God

How do I know what God wants me to do? How can I make decisions that are in line with his will? If God still speaks, will I recognize his voice?

These are important questions, and many Christians grapple with them.

Guidance and the Voice of God charts a way through these often confusing issues, and shows how for those who have ears to hear, God is still speaking loud and clear through his Son.

FOR MORE INFORMATION OR TO ORDER CONTACT:

Matthias Media
sales@matthiasmedia.com.au
matthiasmedia.com.au

Matthias Media (USA)
sales@matthiasmedia.com
matthiasmedia.com

Also by Phillip Jensen

Prayer and the Voice of God

Prayer doesn't have to be a mystery or a burden. In this book, Phillip Jensen and Tony Payne open up what God himself says to us in the Scriptures about prayer, including what prayer really is, why we should do it and why we often don't.

This insightful, practical book offers powerful motivations to get us back on our knees and praying, as well as helpful discussions of what to pray for.

This is a clear, readable guide for new Christians wanting to get started in prayer, or longer-serving Christians whose prayer-lives are wilting.

FOR MORE INFORMATION OR TO ORDER CONTACT:

Matthias Media
sales@matthiasmedia.com.au
matthiasmedia.com.au

Matthias Media (USA)
sales@matthiasmedia.com
matthiasmedia.com

www.ingramcontent.com/pod-product-compliance
Lightning Source LLC
Chambersburg PA
CBHW030220170426
43194CB00007BA/807